MY
heart cried
ENOUGH

MY
heart cried
ENOUGH

Why me Lord?

Marylin Trent

Library of Congress Cataloging-in-Publication Data is available.
ISBN: 979-8-88738-501-3
E-ISBN: 979-8-88738-502-0

From molestation, rape, abuse, and domestic violence to healing, restoration, and victory through Jesus Christ our Lord

TRIBUTE TO MY PARENTS, HALEY F. TRENT AND MARY LOU MORGAN TRENT

The Bible declares that parents are worthy of honor. I am thankful for the love and acceptance my parents so devotedly gave to me. I was an only child for ten years before my brother was born. My parents always called me their little girl and their precious little angel God gave them. They were very attentive to me making sure I learned about Jesus.

Sometimes I went to work with my dad, and he called me his little helper. He was always witnessing to others around him. He carried a New Testament in his pocket so he could always share the gospel of Jesus with others. Sometimes I would go to work with my mom, and she called me her little shadow of love that was always with her. She also shared about Jesus with others we came into contact with. She loved children and would always tell them about Jesus. I remember going to tent revivals with my parents and visiting missionary friends and taking them supplies in Mexico. My dad was an interim pastor for small country churches while the pastoral position was vacant due to pastors retiring, etc. My mom had the voice of an angel, and when she sang, many said it was like listening to an angel singing in heaven. I would accompany her on the piano, and I loved being part of her team as she was invited to sing in many churches. Those were very special memories. I was blessed to have two beautiful parents supporting me, loving me, and teaching me about God and His son.

My mother's last words to me were, "I am blessed and honored God chose me to be your mother. He showed me when you were five years old that you were going to be in ministry and share the gospel with others. My purpose in life was to give birth to you and teach you about Jesus to prepare you to do God's work. You have fulfilled that purpose, and I want you to always keep God and Jesus as your main focus. I love you, and I am honored and highly favored to have been chosen to be your mom." I was so touched by those precious words spoken to me, and I will cherish those words forever.

My father's last words were, "I am very proud that you are my daughter. You have always had a special place in my heart. I have a request: I want you to do the service at my funeral." I told my dad, "Please do not ask me to do this; I do not think I can." He said to me, "You are my daughter, and I do not trust anyone else to do my service. I would not ask you to do this if I was not sure you could not handle it. I know you; you are part of me, and I know without a doubt you are strong and can do my service. I would appreciate you doing this for me." I promised him I would do the service. When he passed, I kept that promise. I did the Roman Road message, and a couple of months after the funeral, I found in his Bible a note stating he wanted the Roman Road message at his funeral. I knew at that moment why he asked me to do his service. We were very close, and he always called me his little girl, even when I was grown. He knew me well.

My way of honoring my parents is by living life to the fullest and remembering all the times they taught me about Jesus and the special memories we have together. I wrote *My Heart Cried Enough* in the 1990s and shared all about my abuse with them and promised both of them I would get it published. Today I fulfill that promise and pray lives will be touched and will find hope, healing, and restoration. Thank you, Mom and Dad, for giving me the truth of the Word of God throughout my life and loving me and encouraging me to always follow my heart for Christ. I love you, and I am honored to have been blessed with two beautiful parents. Thank you for your love for Jesus and your guidance in my life. I know you are in heaven rejoicing with the angels. I love you and miss you. I am looking forward to the day we meet again. To God be the glory!

Your daughter, Marylin

DEDICATION

This book is dedicated to the many women, children, and men who have endured and suffered the torment, devastation, despair, and hurt of abuse and violence. They believe there is no way out as they experience a feeling of loss in many areas of their lives. The loss of self-esteem, emotional stability, self-worth, self-confidence, freedom, trust, identity, friendship, safety, self-respect, hope, optimism, self-assurance, faith, and feeling loved, protected, nurtured, cherished, mental stability, financial stability, and a sense of comfort, joy, peace, a sound mind, and security. All of these areas of loss can be devastating. This book is also dedicated to the children suffering from feeling the chaos is all their fault and feeling alone and abandoned even though their parents are with them in the home. This book is dedicated to the many who feel broken in spirit, the downhearted, and those who struggle to find *hope* and a future awaiting a pathway providing love, acceptance, security, restoration, and victory in life.

ACKNOWLEDGMENTS

I am grateful to my daughter, Hayley Michelle Laughter, for the many hours of endurance in helping to retrieve the book that was written in the mid to late 1990s and lost due to a lightning storm that destroyed the hard drive the manuscript was on. I had a copy of the book saved on a flash drive, and she worked tirelessly converting the manuscript from a Microsoft Works Program to a Microsoft Word Program. I could not have done this endeavor of sharing my story without the support, love, and encouragement my children have given to me. My deepest gratitude to my son, Stacy Lyn Bozarth, and my daughter, Hayley Michelle Laughter, for their generosity in supporting and encouraging me to publish *My Heart Cried Enough*. They lived, survived, and thrived through the chaos of domestic violence, and their love and commitment have been instrumental to the writing of this book. I am truly blessed to have them in my life.

I would like to thank the numerous teams which have given abundant support and encouragement, and hours of intercessory prayer throughout the writing and publication of this book. Thank you to my longtime friend and confidant, Genett Upton of Grace, Mercy, and Joy Ministries, who has faithfully stood beside me and been there for my children and me throughout years of abuse and domestic violence, and for her encouragement, advice, prayers, and helping me through this process, I am sincerely appreciative to Dr. Alberta Helton of Apostolic Ministry, and Alberta Helton Ministries, for her intercessory prayer, love, dedication, and encouragement. I would like to recognize and thank Apostle Ezra Randall, Covenant Kingdom Ministries, for daily intercessory prayer, for his kindness, for the gift of his time, support, encouragement, and guidance, and especially for his mentorship in helping to establish Embracing Restoration Ministries Int'l Inc. and for his abundant advice.

I would also like to thank Jan Crouch, Trinity Broadcasting Network (TBN Ministry), for encouraging me to complete authoring the book and publish the book in the future. In the late 1990s, I had written Jan and shared my desire to help others going through similar experiences in life. I was in the process of drafting a manuscript and needed prayer regarding sharing my testimony, which was difficult to open up about my life journeys. I wrote a summary of the content of the manuscript in progress. She so lovingly and caringly responded and encouraged me to author the book because she felt it would help other women in an analogous situation. Her response is the reason I had the courage to move forward with the book. I know she has received many blessings and rewards for her love and kindness for others. The world is a better place because of her love for Jesus and her sharing the gospel with many nations. What a great legacy she brought to a hurting world and left for years to come. I am profoundly grateful!

I would like to thank my publishing team for all their help and support in this endeavor. My project manager, Jessi Gill, has been very encouraging, helpful, patient, kind, and supportive. I am a first-time author, and her guidance through each phase and step of this project has been rewarding and challenging. I could not have accomplished this without her faithfulness, expertise, and professionalism. She has been a great blessing throughout this project.

I would also like to thank Rhett Harwell for his many phone calls in getting this project to the publishing team and for his guidance to fulfill my dream/vision God planted in my heart to share my life journey in the book, *My Heart Cried Enough*. When I was in the early stages of this endeavor, his sweet spirit of encouragement to go forward helped to bring this passion to reality. Thank you, Rhett!

Thank you to the WorldMissionMedia publishing team for the expertise in the editing process and the suggestions for the completion of this project. Thank you for your patience with me in getting the edits back to you. Your efforts are greatly appreciated. I am grateful to all involved in this process.

Thank you, Trilogy Publishing Team! I am blessed to be a part of the TBN family. Thank you for giving me the opportunity to publish my life journeys in the book *My Heart Cried Enough*.

Thank you to Bridget Blood Photo and Video and Rose Rock Productions for family photos included in *My Heart Cried Enough*.

Thank you, Jesus, for giving me the courage to share my story. And a special "thank you" to Jan Crouch for the encouraging words that helped me to go forward with finishing the manuscript and sharing my story. Many blessings to everyone who took a part in this project!

To God be the glory!

ENDORSEMENTS

The book "My Heart Cried Enough" provided tools to help me walk through forgiveness towards two abusers in my family. I realized I needed to forgive them to be set free from the abuse that was keeping me from having joy and happiness. I realized I had to give my hurts to God and let Him handle the ones who abused me. The bondage of being the victim has been broken. I now have peace. Powerful book.

—Susan Devers

Marylin Trent has a passion for others to overcome hurts, traumas, and unforgiveness that have hindered one's progress in life. Enough is enough. Jesus is our hope. Marylin has revelation that shall help others who have experienced the pain of hopelessness. They shall find the forgiveness and the love of God where the victim becomes victorious!"

—Dr. Alberta Helton,

Alberta Helton Ministries

"My Heart Cried Enough" by Marylin Trent is a powerful and moving story of one woman's journey through unimaginable abuse and trauma and her unwavering faith in God that carried her through to healing and victory. With honesty and vulnerability, Marylin shares her struggles with shame, low self-esteem, and the lies of the enemy and how God helped her to overcome and find true freedom. This book offers hope and encouragement to anyone who has experienced abuse and shows that there is a way to be delivered from the pain and hurt and find new life in Jesus Christ. Trent's *story is a testament to the power of God's love and grace, and a reminder that no matter what life throws our way, we can overcome through Him.*

— Lead Pastor Josh Laughter

The Good Fight Church, Yukon, Oklahoma

TABLE OF CONTENTS

INTRODUCTION

When we go through life's storms, we can feel life has been unfair. Taking us through deep valleys of despair, damaged emotions, depression, hurt, low self-esteem, and chastisement crying out to God for help and direction, thus contemplating the question, "Why has my life been so hard, and why have I walked through so many trials and hardships leading through so many dark places?" Additionally asking the questions, "Why me, Lord?" "What have I done to deserve this pain and heartache?" "Why has my life been so difficult?" There are so many unanswered questions to ponder.

The answers to these questions took years to process, and the storms in my life have proven to be pivotal times of spiritual growth as I have clung to the Lord for peace and strength. My sole desire is to share what the Lord has taught me in hopes that others will find encouragement through God's Word. I found that these questions I pondered reflect God's challenges to my inner being, my heart, my thoughts, and my life. However, some of the storms in my life were of my own making, although I did not understand that concept due to looking at life through my damaged emotions and pain. As you reflect upon questions presented in this book, I pray you will listen to God's voice, the right voice, and meditate upon the scriptures provided in the text of this book.

It is important to have a close relationship with God by listening to what He is calling us to do. Satan's greatest tactic is to make us feel worthless. I know from my experiences and journeys in life, after hearing over and over how horrible I was or that I was not even a Christian. I was told I was full of false doctrine (spiritual abuse), I was contaminated by the world, and that my belief system was corrupted. These words caused me to question where I was in Christ. Thankfully, I listened to God's voice, sharing with me I was made in His image, and God began to show me the truth. I remember this day. Even though I had been involved in ministry for years, the enemy had a plan to take me out of ministry. God has a purpose and plan for each and every person who will subject themselves to the obedience of God's Word and plan for our lives. Jeremiah 29:11 (NIV), "For I know the plans I have for you, declares the Lord, plans to prosper you and not to harm you, plans to give you a hope and a future." How great is our God! We must realize that we are not worthless. We are important to Him; He has work for us to do for Him! So, we must listen to what voices, words, and actions, are being spoken to us, over us, or at us from someone else. If something is going on in life that is blocking us from hearing God's voice, we must clear it from our life. We must call upon God in these moments and repent of accepting the tricks of the enemy in our lives and ask the Lord to restore our relationship with God our Father and his Son Jesus Christ. The more time we spend listening to God's voice and not receiving what the enemy says about us, the closer our relationship will be with God, and *we will overcome*. Words have power. Their meaning creates perceptions that shape our beliefs about self and drive our behaviors which creates the world around us. We must walk with God and break the curse the enemy puts upon us.

My Heart Cried Enough is a story about my life journey through abuse and how God has been there, holding me up each step of the way. The most important chapter is when God took me through the forgiveness process. I had prayed and asked God if there was anyone I needed to forgive. The Holy Spirit brought to my mind (twenty-six) people I needed to forgive. This was a huge process for my understanding of why I needed to forgive them. They were the perpetrator—*they* should be asking for forgiveness for their actions.

Lovingly, God was with me all the time. He later showed me how He held my spirit above the abuse, trauma, pain, lies, deception, hurt, anger, and manipulation and how Satan and his servants devised plans and used mankind to attempt to destroy and betray me and come against me. Satan's purpose in life is to "steal, kill and destroy" our lives, joy, peace, trust, emotions, and mental stability.

There are many men and women suffering the consequences of abuse and domestic violence, and they believe there is no way out and a feeling of no hope for a decent quality of life. However, through Jesus Christ, there *is* a way to be delivered from shame, false guilt, low self-esteem, and damaged emotions and find that all the hurt can be turned around for good, resulting in victory. The change is the victim becomes victorious through Christ! Then, and only then, can we have love, acceptance, redemption, grace, mercy, forgiveness, and a sound mind!

One day my heart cried out to God, and I told Him very sternly, "I cannot take anymore." I "demanded" if I was truly His daughter, for Him to take me out of this world. Well, He did not answer "my demand," and I am still here, thirty-plus years later, and I know I am truly His daughter. He promised never to leave me or forsake me, and He has faithfully kept that promise. He saw me through physical, sexual, emotional, verbal, financial, and spiritual abuse, torment, shame, false guilt, unforgiveness, and low self-esteem. When I asked, "Why me, Lord? What have I done to deserve all this pain and destruction?" That was the day "my heart cried enough," and God began taking me through the numerous journeys of healing and forgiveness, showing me how strong in Him I truly was. When I asked Him why He allowed *me* to go through this suffering, He gently told me, "Marylin, my precious child, I knew you were strong enough in Me to survive, and I knew you would tell others how you overcame being a victim, how you survived and thrived. I knew you would make it through many journeys of life, and in the end, you would give Me (God) and My Son, Jesus Christ, all the *glory* for an abundant life." He was, even to me, invisible at times, not seeing Him there through the pain, trauma, and suffering. However, He was my strength, my life, my help, my determination, my endurance, my rock, and my all. He has done miraculous things for me, and He has been there every step through my many journeys.

Satan could *try* to destroy my flesh and emotions and even, at times, crush my spirit, but *God is God!* God showed me how He held my spirit above the abuse and that Satan really had *no* power over my spirit, my will, and my life on earth and eternally.

Where God and His Son, Jesus, reside, there is life, and death cannot touch me physically or spiritually. Satan has lost the battle for my life. We can overcome his evil tactics, thus seeing the truth for what it is (whom we are really fighting/the principalities of the air—not flesh and blood). Then, we know and believe, "No weapon formed against us can ever prosper!" (Isaiah 54:17, KJV). Amen!

I no longer have shame, false guilt, low self-esteem, damaged emotions, or doubt; I am aware of the tricks/wiles of the enemy that he uses to try to destroy me. He attempts to fight me all the time; however, I serve Yeshua, the son of God, who has already defeated the enemy at the cross. Satan is a defeated foe and has no power over me. His days are numbered. He is crushed, a failure, pressed down, and he can no longer torment my spirit, soul, or body. What can he do to me? Nothing that God does not allow. Like Job, God allowed Satan to take everything from him but not his life. I know the story of Job well. I have lived it. I have victory through Jesus Christ and want others to know they have hope because Jesus *is* the way, the truth, and *the life!* Second Corinthians 5:17, "Therefore, if anyone is in Christ, He is a new creation, the old has gone, the new has come!" Amen.

My Heart Cried Enough is a story of my journeys from rape, molestation, emotional abuse, physical abuse, sexual abuse, verbal abuse, financial abuse, spiritual abuse, unforgiveness, and working through shame, false guilt, low self-esteem, pain, hurt, anger, and all facets of abuse, lovingly taking me through forgiveness, giving me a sound mind, joy, happiness, healing, deliverance, and victory! Victory is ahead for the victim and the perpetrator, which is who Jesus died for—everyone. We all need Jesus, and the truth needs to be shared for others to know there is a way to overcome with great power through Jesus Christ, the Son of God!

The pages of this book were God-given to this writer to offer encouragement to learn to be still and listen to God's voice deep within my soul and learn to recognize the lies of the enemy. It took me years to process my feelings through the many acts of violence, abuse, condemnation, and false beliefs of self, and in the pages of this book, I pray for the healing of many who have endured all the enemy has designed and planned to destroy beautiful lives that God has destined for an abundant life. Walking through trials and hardships is extremely difficult. However, the storms and journeys in my life have proven to be a journey of healing. My desire is to pass on what the Lord has taught me in hopes that you also might be encouraged by God's Word.

This book is dedicated to numerous victims who feel broken in spirit, the downhearted, and those who are in need of finding the path to have hope and a future awaiting their victory in life.

To God be the glory!

Marylin Trent

CHAPTER ONE

The Lost Journey:
"Unanswered Questions"

One cool, brisk fall morning, I was driving to work praying to God. I asked Him why so many terrible things had happened in my life. Had I done something wrong, or was the world we live in unusually cruel? As I pondered this thought, I became angry and demanded that God take me out of this horrible world. If I was really His child and He loved me, why would He allow all of these traumatic things to happen to "His child"? David expressed his anger and anxiety with the Lord because he felt abandoned by Him. Psalm 42:9 (Zondervan Life Application Bible), "I say to God my Rock, why have you forgotten me? Why must I go about mourning, oppressed by the Enemy?" And David prayed to God in Psalm 142:1–7,

> I cry aloud to the Lord; I lift up my voice to the Lord for mercy. I pour out my complaint before him; before him, I tell my trouble. When my spirit grows faint within me, it is you who know my way. In the path where I walk men have hidden a snare for me. Look to my right and see; no one is concerned for me. I have no refuge; no one cares for my life. I cry to you, O Lord; I say, You are my refuge, my portion in the land of the living. Listen to my cry, for I am in desperate need: rescue me from those who pursue me, for they are too strong for me, Set me free from my prison, that I may praise your name.
>
> Psalm 142:1–7 (Zondervan Life Application Bible)

I could relate to David's feelings. Where was my Father when I needed him? Even His Son, Jesus Christ, asked of His Father, "My God, my God, why have you forsaken me?" (Matthew 27:46, Zondervan Life Application Bible). While forsaken expresses loneliness, we may lose our sense of God's presence but not our trust. Christ knew God had not left him, but at that time of darkness, Jesus expressed his feelings. As I experienced heaviness, loneliness, anxiety, fear, and rejection, I pounded on the steering wheel and yelled emphatically, "Take me out of this world now! I don't care how; send a truck or whatever it takes, just take me out." David also cried out to God regarding his despair about difficult situations. Psalm 55:4–5 (Zondervan Life Application Bible): "My heart is in anguish within me; the terrors of death assail me. Fear and trembling have beset me; horror has overwhelmed me." David was not afraid to come to God and express his true feelings and needs. God wants us to be honest with Him about all of our emotions, not just pleasant ones. I began sobbing as the hurt inside of me burst forth. The only answer I received was the echoing of my own voice in the car. In my heart, I knew I should not misjudge the "silence" of God for the absence of God. God knew every abuse that had been inflicted upon me. I later knew that God was with me, even during my times of suffering. I was reminded that Jesus had endured and suffered more than I could ever endure in a lifetime. However, the brokenness of my spirit and heart could not understand this at this season of my life. (This will be discussed more in another chapter.)

Thankfully, God did not honor my request, and I arrived safely at the business where I was employed. Apathetically I opened the door to my office and sat at my desk to begin the day's work. The lady who worked in the office with me was looking upward at the ceiling. She said she could see a glimmering light above my head reflecting the shape of a dove. As

I observed the glowing light, I acknowledged affirmatively that it did look like a dove. I felt as if the Holy Spirit was hovering directly above my head. I knew at this moment that God was watching over me, lovingly letting me know that He really cared for me. I felt at peace in God's love. That was His way of telling me, "I am here for you. Do not be afraid of things you do not understand. I will never leave you or forsake you. You are my child, and I will give you the strength to overcome. I have a plan for your life, so do not be dismayed." David knew that God cared for him, as he said in Psalm 72:12–14 (Zondervan Life Application Bible), "For he will deliver the needy who cry out, the afflicted who have no one to help. He will take pity on the weak and the needy and save the needy from death. He will rescue them from oppression and violence, for precious is their blood in his sight." The Word of God is a relational teaching tool to help us through any emotion or situation we are experiencing.

God's Word is true, and we can learn how others cried out to God in their distress and find comfort through their experiences, thus helping us not to feel alone. We can always trust God because God tells us in His Word in Psalm 46:1 (Zondervan Life Application Bible), "God is our refuge and strength, an ever-present help in trouble."

Early in my life, I had gone through many painful situations, and the hurts had left me devastated and damaged. One could say that my spirit had been broken; I no longer felt whole. I felt weakened and destroyed by all the hurts and traumas, left with a sense of being damaged, shattered, destroyed, defective, and without hope. I was emotionally injured, and I was tired of suffering. Zondervan's Life Application Bible dictionary/concordance defines "broken" as "fractured or shattered; violated or transgressed against." I had been abused in many distinctive ways until I felt I could not take any more. I was crushed, and my trust in mankind had been destroyed. I felt worthless and infinitely damaged, believing no one really cared. I needed restoration from the experiences forced upon me within a sinful world.

I needed love, security, and acceptance from a world that had rejected me. I felt I had failed according to society's standards. However, the person doing the rejection is the one with the problem, causing others to be injured emotionally and mentally and devalued in many other ways. Satan wants us to walk around feeling defeated. Therefore, we must reject Satan's lies and accept God's view of us. God tells us in Psalm 34:18, "The Lord is close to the brokenhearted and saves those who are crushed in spirit." God is faithful when we feel the need to escape our pain, loss, failures, and hurtful situations.

For that reason, we must realize God, Jesus Christ, and the Holy Spirit are the only true sources of strength and power for restoration. "He heals the brokenhearted and binds up their wounds" (Psalm 147:3). Jesus was perfect in every aspect of the word; however, He was rejected, despised, abused, and wounded by mankind's cruel words and actions. Just as Satan became jealous of God and later wanted Christ to be destroyed, he also has the desire to destroy us. We may be broken from abuse, but we can be restored through Christ and His example. God will provide a way out of the pain. In his song "Trading My Sorrows," Darrell Evans sings, "I'm trading my sorrows, I'm trading my shame; I'm laying them down for the joy of the Lord. I'm trading my sickness, I'm trading my pain, I'm laying them down for the joy of the Lord. I am pressed but not crushed, persecuted not abandoned, struck down but not destroyed, I am blessed beyond the curse for His promise will endure and His joy is gonna' be my strength, though sorrow may last for the night; the joy comes with the morning." Therefore, we have a choice to say yes to our Lord and begin a new day in Him or end up living in our past and being hurt forever. Psalm 30:5 (Zondervan Life Application Bible), "For His anger lasts only a moment, but His favor lasts a lifetime; weeping may remain for a night, but rejoicing comes in the morning."

I had reached the point in my life where everything was beginning to surface, and I knew I needed to talk to someone. I prayed that God would show me who because I did not understand my feelings. Why was I crying so much? Why was I hurting? I needed answers to these questions. Jesus assures us in His Word that "He will wipe every tear from their eyes. There will be no more death or mourning or crying or pain, for the old order of things have passed away" (Revelation 21:4, Zondervan Life Application Bible). I did not understand my weeping, my feelings, the hurt, and the pain.

In spite of my doubts and fears, Jesus heard my cry for help. Jesus knew all I had to do was cry out to Him. "Call to me and I will answer you and tell you great and unsearchable things you do not know" (Jeremiah 33:3, Zondervan Life Application Bible).

When the deepest part of my being cried out to Him, He responded to me in His love, mercy, and compassion, and during these deep sorrows, I could not see His hand upon me; however, I knew in my heart that I could trust Him through it all! I know His love for me is what helped me survive. Psalm 46:1 (NIV): "God is our refuge and strength, an ever-present help in trouble."

I had met a wonderful lady in a hospital waiting room several years prior when my ten-year-old daughter was having surgery. Little did I know at the time she was going to be a very instrumental part in helping me to work through the many years of deep-rooted pain and abuse. God brought her name to my mind twelve years after meeting her in that hospital waiting area; however, I had lost her phone number. I knew I needed to talk to someone because I had been crying nonstop for three weeks, not understanding why I was sobbing so much.

God kept bringing her name to my mind. I could not locate her. I called the operator and asked for her telephone number, but unfortunately, her number was an unlisted number. The telephone operator said she was not allowed to give out her information. A few minutes later, the telephone operator called me back and asked me if she called Delta, would it be okay to give her my phone number. She stated she was going against policy to do this, but the Lord prompted her to try and reach her for me. She called "Delta" and explained to her I was trying to reach her, but I had lost her phone number. She gave Delta my name and number, and she contacted me giving me the opportunity to share with her. She asked me if I was able to drive to Edmond, Oklahoma, and I responded yes. She cleared her schedule for the afternoon, and I was at her home in about an hour. She was a Christian therapist, and this day began a two-year process of working through the numerous circumstances that had left me emotionally crushed and damaged. Under her guidance, I remembered many things that I had repressed. She was my miracle that began the unfolding process of the many wounds embedded in my inner being. I needed the guidance of my therapist to accept the things in my life that I could not change. I learned that I was not a bad person. I was simply a victim of someone else's pain and wrong choices.

As I remembered many painful circumstances in my life, I realized one of the strongest emotions I felt at this time was anger. God does not want us to live in pain and anger. This pain can become a sin if we do not let it go. Pain is simply hurting. She taught me that hurt could turn to anger, and anger could turn to revenge or bitterness. Anger can be directed toward self, others, or both leading to depression, destructive actions, and even psychosomatic symptoms.

God's Word tells us in Ephesians 4:26 (NIV), "In your anger do not sin. Do not let the sun go down while you are still angry, and do not give the devil a foothold." It is okay to be angry; nevertheless, we should not allow this anger to become sin. Anger is usually our most common response to rejection. We are accountable for controlling our anger and dealing with it in an appropriate manner. The solution to anger and bitterness is *forgiveness*. We must be honest with God, and ourselves, about our anger. If we don't resolve our anger through honesty and forgiveness, we can become resentful and bitter. We must confess our sins to God. The sin of carrying the pain and not letting it go. This is the only way we can work through this feeling of anger. We must release it and let it go. It is imperative that we forgive ourselves and others. (I will share more about forgiveness in a later chapter.)

Isaiah 61 tells us that Jesus came to heal the brokenhearted. I believe this refers to those who have been hurt (broken inside), those whose spirits have been crushed and wounded. This deep brokenness inside of us must be healed. God says that His kingdom is within us in Luke 17:21. Also, Romans 14:1 tells us that the kingdom of God is righteousness, peace, and joy in the Holy Spirit, who gives us hope and a promise for inner healing.

No matter what circumstances evolve in our lives, we can be whole through Jesus Christ because He is the King of God's kingdom. His presence will help us to survive and give us the means to enjoy life. Jesus is the way, the truth, and the life. We are strengthened in our hearts, mind, and will through the power of the Holy Spirit. Zondervan Life Application Bible states in Ephesians 3:16, 17a, "He may strengthen you with power through His Spirit in your inner being, so that Christ may dwell in your hearts through Faith." And in Zechariah 4:6 (NIV), "Not by might, nor by power, but by my Spirit says the Lord Almighty."

We must remember that survival from traumatic events in life comes from obedience to God, praying for God's will over us, and asking daily for inner strength through Jesus Christ and God's Word. When we listen to the Holy Spirit, we will be dedicated and devoted to God by being separated from sin.

It is only through God and His Son, Jesus Christ, that anything of lasting value is accomplished. We should not trust in our own strengths or our own abilities. The principle of life is to depend on God and allow the Holy Spirit to work in and through us. God rejoices in what is right, not what is big. We must be faithful in the small things to be successful in the bigger opportunities He places before us. We must begin where we currently are and be faithful to what is before us now and leave the results to God. God's first command is to "Love the Lord your God with all your heart and with all your soul and with all your mind. This is the first and greatest commandment. And the second is like it: Love your neighbor as yourself" (Matthew 22:37–39, Zondervan Life Application Bible). This is a great place to begin in our lives.

We cannot love our neighbors if we do not love ourselves. First, we need to apply the strength of God and Jesus Christ to our lives and then extend the strength of God and His Son, Jesus, into others' lives. We cannot give love if we do not have a love for God, Jesus Christ, and ourselves.

Salvation is not enough to carry us through feelings of low self-esteem, anger, betrayal, hurt, bitterness, weakness, confusion, sadness, and other struggles we may be experiencing. We must surrender *all* to Christ. This requires great mental and emotional energy as well as determination. We must never give up. "We need to be transformed (the work of change through the Holy Spirit and God's Word) by the renewing of our minds" (Romans 12:2, KJV).

The fact that we feel pain from our past is not a sign of a failed relationship with God. The presence of pain does not mean that we do not have salvation in our lives. This is what the enemy wants us to believe. Pain is simply a signal telling us we need to begin the process of healing by daily depending on the Holy Spirit to guide our thoughts, actions, and will. Jesus will bring the healing and make the necessary changes. First, we must admit that the pain and problems in our lives are real, and we must reach out to God and Jesus and confess where we currently are. The Bible has many accounts of men and women who struggled to overcome their circumstances, trials, and temptations. It took effort to work through these situations. We can study these examples, apply them to our own lives and learn to appreciate the core value of these representations and solutions in God's powerful, sustaining Word. I had to depend on Jesus to take me through the healing process, but I also needed the assistance of a Christian therapist to unfold the locked memories deep inside my soul. I know that God alone could have provided those steps; however, God and His Son, Jesus, know each one of us intimately, and they know what and who we need in our lives to help us. God provided the expertise in a wonderful Christian woman to stand beside me and walk me through those painful memories. Pray and seek the wisdom and guidance of the Holy Spirit for your own situation. What worked for me may not totally work for you. I do know that it took God and Jesus Christ to obtain my total and complete healing. I could not have been healed by therapy alone.

However, Jesus alone could have healed me. For me, it took both to acquire my freedom from my past. Seek God first, and the rest will fall into place.

> I will lead the blind by ways they have not known, along unfamiliar paths I will guide them; I will turn the darkness into light before them and make the rough places smooth. These are the things I will do, I will not forsake them.
>
> Isaiah 42:16 (NIV)

CHAPTER TWO
The Journey Through: "Feelings"

S ome of the terms Webster's 1913 Dictionary uses to define "abuse" are: "misuse; use for a wrong purpose; improper or unfair treatment; to hurt by treating badly, maltreat, to dishonor, violate, deceive, to offend, hurt, insulting speech, (to use insulting, coarse, or bad language about or to someone); a bad unjust or corrupt custom or practice, crime." Also, my therapist told me that abuse means to injure and that violence and abuse mirror each other due to both implementing fear and/or control over the victim.

I had to uncover all the events of abuse (physical, verbal, emotional, mental, spiritual, financial, and sexual) that brought me to the point of anger, frustration, fear, broken relationships, abandonment, false accusations, a conflicting belief system, exclusion from groups, ridicule, condemnation, and judgmental conduct by some Christian views, and many other hurtful actions. My first step to healing came throughout the long-term sessions of therapy. During this time, I authored a poem titled "I Can't Heal What I Can't Feel." This poem revealed how much I had shut down in my life.

"I Can't Heal What I Can't Feel"

I can't heal what I can't feel

But what I don't feel—feels so very real.

I have inside me feelings that are churning,

No healing have I, but within, I am yearning.

For the blessings of life—being able to live again,

And have feelings and passion so deep within.

At this moment, I don't have stability inside,

I have so much hurt and pain I feel I have to hide.

If I could only feel what I felt years ago,

I feel I would have a chance to again be whole.

I want to be happy from this day forward and until
I'm old,

Resulting with passion inside my heart that can't be
bought with gold.

I know I can't heal if I don't let myself feel,

I really want to feel so I can have the will

To be happy and whole, and my life set free,

Thus, knowing that "feeling, living and loving" are
the keys.

When the heartaches of my past

Are gone from me at last

Then and only then can I begin to heal,

Finding passion and feeling what is real.

My life has been filled with too many heartaches;

It is time for the sun to rise at daybreak!

If I can only heal my soul and let the worst be done;

Then, my battle will be over, and my inner war will
be won!

(Marylin Trent, 1991)

I started drafting this poem one morning before the sun started coming over the horizon. God showed me that as the sun began to rise, it was time for the light to come back into my life. Some people allow their feelings to turn them away from God and His Son, Jesus Christ, while others allow their feelings to find hope in God, remembering His goodness. During such times, living by faith takes on a new meaning. We must learn to trust what we cannot feel or see. "By day the Lord directs His love, at night His song is with me—a prayer to the God of my life" (Psalm 42:8, Zondervan Life Application Bible).

It is important to learn to listen to the voice of the Holy

Spirit because the Holy Spirit is our Counselor, Comforter, Helper, Intercessor, Advocate, Strengthener, Guide, and Teacher. The Holy Spirit convicts and will never misguide us. It is so vitally important to have a personal relationship with God our Father, His Son, Jesus, and the Holy Spirit. John 10:27–28 (Zondervan's Life Application Bible), "My sheep know my voice; I know them, and they follow me. I give them eternal life, and they shall never perish; no one can snatch them out of my hand." We must give the Holy Spirit a chance to work in our lives daily.

Another poem I wrote within four days of the previously mentioned one spoke volumes to me about listening to God, the Holy Spirit, and Jesus Christ.

"The Voice Within"

Let us be silent

that we may hear God's voice in our souls.

Only then can we be guided

and directed to become completely whole.

As we are still and listen to our inner voice

we will surely be inspired.

Aiming to communicate with the inner presence

of living and fulfilling our deepest desires.

As we continue to listen and respond

to this inner voice—a new life will begin.

We will be in touch with our passion, thus

allowing us to release our joys from within.

Soon we will find ourselves flowing with creativity,
dreams, and strength,

discovering we can be what we were really meant to be.

This experience is essential to finding inner peace

and, therefore, reveals to the heart what the heart is ready
to receive.

The beauty through God's Word gives us the power

to separate from the outside forces that cause dismay,

And as we listen to the Holy Spirit, we are guided and
directed to make perfect our way.

So, let us be silent

that we may hear the Holy Spirit in our souls,

Only then can we be guided

and directed to become completely whole.

(Marylin Trent, 1991)

We go through many stages of healing. We must work
through the pain to appreciate and recognize growth and healing. God knows each of us intimately; therefore, He guides us

through the steps that will help us recover from life's harrowing tragedies. God knew my heart, and He knew I could take these distressing situations I endured and turn them around for good by helping others who suffer and experience abuse. He showed me how to deepen my relationship with Him by giving me knowledge and wisdom to overcome and move to a higher level through Him.

Part of my healing was the moment "my heart cried enough," materializing in the form of anger toward God because I felt as if He had forsaken me and did not care. I needed answers, so God provided the necessary tools to open doors for the process of my understanding.

To help identify your feelings, answer the following questions.

Have you ever wanted God to take you out of this world?

_____

_____

_____

_____

_____

Why?

_____

_____

_____

_____

Have you experienced any traumatic situations/circumstances?

_____

_____

_____

_____

_____

Name them.

_____

_____

_____

_____

Why do you think God allows traumatic things to happen to us?

_____

_____

_____

_____

Where do you think God is during our abuse and pain?

_____

_____

_____

Have you ever asked God the "why" question, and you don't get answers?

_____

_____

_____

_____

_____

It all began in a small town one Saturday in May. I was born at home, where my grandmother and the physician collaborated trying to get me to breathe. There was a battle that was raging for my life, but God had a plan. God tells us in Jeremiah 29:11 (Zondervan Life Application Bible), "'For I know the plans I have for you,' declares the Lord, 'plans to prosper you and not to harm you, plans to give you hope and a future.'" The commentary in Zondervan's Life Application Bible explains this verse very well:

> We're all encouraged by a leader who stirs us to move ahead, someone who believes we can do the task he has given and who will be with us all the way. God is that kind of leader. He knows the future, and His plans for us are good and full of *hope*. As long as God, who knows the future, provides our agenda and goes with us as we fulfill his mission, we can have boundless hope. This does not mean that we will be spared pain, suffering, or hardship but that God will see us through to a glorious conclusion.

God never left me, but through the cloudiness of the painful events, I could not see clearly. I learned that I should commit to accepting the fact that I can no longer make excuses for the way my life was going. I am obligated to observe my thoughts, behaviors, and feelings and find new ways to combat the way I deal with the situations that have crossed my path. This requires humility to accept guidance. I knew God was there, but I was unable to recognize the guidance He offered me.

The hurt and pain were so deeply implanted that my vision was blinded. I had gone through the steps of remembering all of the past traumatic situations, and now my spirit needed to be healed. This was a very extensive and challenging process. The embedded roots of pain and hurt needed to be pruned and dug out, so I could have an abundant life. "The enemy (the destroyer) comes to kill, steal and destroy our lives" (John 10:10a, NIV), but he could not succeed if I trusted God's help through these devastating situations that adversely affected me. Jesus said in John 10:10b (NIV), "I have come that they may have life, and have it to the fullest." This is a powerful promise Christ gives to us. All we have to do is believe His Words and accept His guidance so we can rebuild our spiritual lives. Serving God fully and completely is not based on our feelings.

It is a choice. We choose to trust Him completely or rely on ourselves for strength. We cannot control our lives, as God did not create us to live independently of Him. We are to be dependent on Jesus Christ to live according to God's infinite plan. We must grow daily from level to level (or from glory to glory). Only then can we experience total healing, true peace, and joy. It is definitely a work in progress.

The story of Daniel gave me great insight during this time of my life, and as I studied Daniel, I began to climb toward the top of the mountain, at which point I started to see more clearly. As I was engulfed in sorrow and despair, I felt that God was absent, thus the questions: "Where is God?" "Do I give in to my situations, or do I simply give up?" At this point, I decided I should be courageous and hold on to faith. This is what Daniel did. He was steadfast in praying and crying out to God. He had great faith that God would see him through everything. There he was in the midst of numerous hungry lions, and Daniel had no fear. He continued to pray and believe in God's protection when it looked as though the ferocious lions would devour him. Like Daniel, I felt as though I was being condemned to die. I was in this deep valley of oppression while Daniel was in a den of hungry lions. We have an enemy who has a plan to devour us physically, emotionally, and spiritually. However, Daniel did not waiver in his belief that God would protect him and bring him through what appeared to be an impossible way out of the lion's den. God's ways are different than our ways, and God never fails. He never leaves us or forsakes us, even in the most unbearably difficult circumstances. God will take what life throws at us and turn it all around for good to be used for His Glory! We have to embrace HOPE:

H=Hold on to faith and trust in Him.

O=Obedience to God no matter what our situation is like.

P=Pray and Praise without ceasing in all things.

E=Endure by trusting God to see us through.

Answer these questions in regard to your actions/feelings.

Have there been any circumstances in your life that you felt like God had deserted you?

_____

_____

_____

Name them.

_____

_____

_____

_____

_____

How did you act or react to these situations?

_____

_____

_____

_____

_____

Were you angry, sad, or depressed, or did you not have a reaction at all?

_____

_____

_____

_____

Did your feelings from this situation come at the onset of the situation or later in life?

_____

_____

_____

_____

How did you cope or deal with your situation?

_____

_____

_____

_____

Did you repress your feelings, suppress your feelings, or express your feelings?

_____

_____

_____

_____

Did you cry out to God, praying and keeping your faith in Him?

_____

_____

_____

_____

Delta Wilkinson, my therapist, assigned me these questions and definitions and asked me to think about each category and reflect on how I coped with my situations.

Did I repress, suppress, or express my feelings?

"Repress" means to block something from your mind (hide them so deep that you cannot remember the situation).

"Suppress" means to prevent evidence or information from becoming known; to prevent others from knowing; to restrain or limit the effects (due to shame, embarrassment, fear of rejection or condemnation, unworthiness, or timidity).

"Express" means to say your thoughts or feelings in words (harsh words, anger is directed toward self or others); to convey your feelings through gestures or behaviors (to act out); to make your thoughts or feelings known to others, to act out or to inflict your hurt or pain inwardly toward self or outwardly toward others.

After pondering my situation and realizing I did not remember most of the events in my life, I realized I learned to repress my experiences so deep I could not remember the details of my abuse from childhood. Thus, the reason for needing Delta, my therapist, to help unlock these memories I had buried so deeply. Subsequently, God showed me how He was there for me. I had come to the place I was either going to listen to God or be miserable all my life. I had to find a way to not feel bitter. God showed me the way to not be bitter is to take the "I" out of the word bitter and replace the "I" with an "E" and think about how to make my life better. I had to focus on removing the "I" (me, myself, and I) to have "E" everlasting joy and a better life.

God gave me the opportunity to share my testimony which took a great amount of humility and faith on my part. Little did I know that through this endeavor, God was going to give me more healing and reveal something profound to me. The pastor of the church I was attending told me that I had a special testimony to share, and he would like for me to do this on the following Sunday morning. I thought, *How does he know what I have to express?* God had spoken to him, unaware that God had already shown me that someday I was to share with others what I had been through.

Fear overcame me; therefore, I began to pray and ask God what He wanted me to say. Did he really want me to convey those horrible acts of betrayal? Was church the place to talk about such devastating and demeaning attacks on my life? "Lord," I prayed, "how can I do this? What is the purpose of my sharing this part of my life with others? What will they think of me?" I was terrified of the outcome. I knew I was at a crossroads in my life, and the Lord was challenging me to stretch my faith and trust him 100 percent. He reminded me of a portion of a verse in Revelation 12:11a (KJV), "They overcame him by the blood of the Lamb, and by the word of their testimony..." Needless to say, this was one of the longest weeks of my life. Could I really do this? Would I follow the Lord's leading and take that leap of faith to trust His direction? "When I am afraid, I will trust in you. In God, whose word I praise; In God I trust; I will not be afraid. What can mortal man do to me?" (Psalm 56:3, 11, NIV)

CHAPTER THREE
The Leap of Faith Journey: "The Testimony"

Sunday morning ultimately arrived. I was so nervous, and I thought maybe the pastor would forget he asked me to do this. Although I had jotted down a few scriptures and points of interest, I still did not know what I was going to say. An incredibly special friend was there with me that morning, and she leaned over to me and said, "Trust God, and He will hold you up as you share."

The service began with praise and worship. Then the pastor walked to the podium and said, "This morning, we are having a special lady share her testimony," and he asked me to come forward to the podium. He handed me the microphone, and I felt as though I was going to faint. I silently asked God for direction. The scripture Philippians 4:13 (KJV) came to mind: "I can do all things through Christ who gives me strength." I began sharing what a wonderful God we serve; He loves us unconditionally. He gave His only Son for each and every one of us. We all go through trials, tests, and traumatic circumstances, and sometimes in this process, we suffer hurt, abuse, torment, and pain. We have an enemy who wants to destroy us, especially if we are working to further God's kingdom. Satan is jealous and will stop at nothing to discourage us.

I shared about Christ and what He did for me at a young age, calling me to do ministry for Him, changing me, and giving me eternal life. The enemy wanted to take out a member of God's army, but the battle was won when Jesus died on the cross. I know some people feel that we may give Satan too much credit for what he does, but the Bible tells us there is a war going on in our lives. He (Satan) is very real, and we must acknowledge his evil presence and his tactics if we are going to become victorious. After all, his deceptive, cunning tricks started in the Garden of Eden. We must trust God and daily claim Ephesians 6:10–18 over our lives, our loved ones, and all of God's children. We cannot lose sight of God's promises to keep us safely in His arms. "Thou art my hope in the day of evil" (Jeremiah 17:17, KJV).

The path of the Christian is not always bright with sunshine; we have our seasons of trials, darkness, and storms. Sometimes, we find our Christian life has been covered with clouds, and during these times, we cannot see the light through the haze. Have you ever thought that maybe God has allowed the sun shinny days during our weak and unassertive times? The clouds may hover over us for a season, the times when we are stronger in our spiritual life than we realize. The days of trial help us to strengthen our relationship with Christ. I have endured many traumatic events, but I stand here today as a witness that Satan lost the battle for my life. I have been molested, raped, beaten, and left for dead, abused physically, mentally, verbally, sexually, financially, spiritually, and emotionally. However, I know and love a God who is bigger than all that I have endured. I had questioned God, "Where were you when all this happened to me?" (God revealed to me the answer to this question at that moment). Tears filled my eyes as God gave me an instant vision; while evil was attacking my physical body, God's provision was there in the midst of the attack holding my spirit above the torment. God tells us in His Word, "You gave me life and showed me kindness, and in your providence watched over my spirit" (Job 10:12, Zondervan Life Application Bible). Satan could attack my flesh, but he could not take my life, nor could he touch my spirit. (For a moment, memories of the event were revealed.) I continued to share at the young age of sixteen; throughout the course of this specific attack, I was surrounded by five guys who had assembled to violate me and take my life. Seeing that I was entirely in their hands, I silently asked Jesus for help. During these circumstances that were beyond my control, I clung extremely near to Jesus as He protected my spirit. I took refuge in Him. "You are my hiding place; You will protect me from trouble and surround me with songs of deliverance. I will instruct you and teach you in the way you should go, I will counsel you and watch over you" (Psalm 32:7–8, NIV). At that moment, a mighty healing took place. I knew at that moment God kept His promise to never leave me or forsake me. I felt a peace that passeth all understanding as I shared that event and the revelation God was giving me at that instant. I asked everyone to completely lay their lives in God's hands. He will stand by your side and help you through every situation you have experienced and those you are currently going through. I inquired if there was anyone who had been abused in any way, and a few hands were raised. I affirmed that God, through His Son, Jesus, could carry them through the hurt and pain, and He loved them as they were. Others might see me as damaged, but God sees me as His beautiful precious child and to not believe the lies of the enemy.

Remember Romans 8:1–2 (NIV), "Therefore, there is now no condemnation for those who are in Christ Jesus, because through Christ Jesus the law of the Spirit of life set me free." I voiced at that moment, "If anyone needs prayer, please feel free to come forward, and someone will pray with them." Men, women, and young people came forward. I know God used me as a vessel that morning to reach those who were hurting. As I sat down, my friend "GG" hugged me and said, "Marylin, this is only the beginning. God is going to use your experiences and testimony to help others."

I was not aware a professional in psychology was in the congregation that morning, and after church, he came to me and shared that he was a psychologist for the court system in another state and was visiting family. He shared about others he had counseled that were Christians, and some had described their experiences as similar to mine. They stated they felt like they were above the actual situation, and they were protected in an unexplainable way. He told me he sincerely appreciated my sharing of the event where I was beaten, raped, and left for dead. He enlightened me to "not let the enemy cause doubt because God had protected me. And to stand firm on the vision God gave me, never forgetting what He did for me during the assault."

This was one more step toward my healing. People thanked me for sharing my testimony, gave me hugs, and supported me spiritually and surprisingly unconditionally. God is a formidable God. The shame that Satan tried to put on me was diminished through God's love for me. God opened many doors that day. I was given a scholarship to go to Biblical Counseling School at Vine Life Ministries by a couple that was in the service that morning and later to Scope Ministries in Oklahoma City, Oklahoma. This was the beginning of my training ground to help others who have endured abuse. Psalm 25:1–5 and 15–21 are verses that have given me *hope* and encouragement in my daily walk with Christ.

> To you, O Lord, I lift up my soul; in you, I trust, O my God. Do not let me be put to shame, nor let my enemies' triumph over me. No one whose hope is in you will ever be put to shame, but they will be put to shame who are treacherous without excuse. Show me your ways, O Lord, teach me your paths; guide me in your truth and teach me, for you are my salvation, and my hope is in you all day long.
>
> Psalm 25:1–5 (Zondervan Life Application Bible)

My eyes are ever on the Lord, for only he will release my feet from the snare. Turn to me and be gracious to me, for I am lonely and afflicted. The troubles of my heart have multiplied; free me from my anguish. Look upon my affliction and my distress and take away all my sins. See how my enemies have increased and how fiercely they hate me! Guard my life and rescue me; let me not be put to shame, for I take refuge in you. May integrity and uprightness protect me because my hope is in you.

Psalm 25:15–21
(Zondervan Life Application Bible)

We must remember our *hope* is in Christ. *Hope* is *healing* through the *opportunity* to gain experience by being *persistent* in accepting the things I cannot change and *evaluating* where I am in Christ. I appreciate the definition of *"hope"* in Zondervan's Life Application Bible Concordance, which is "to desire something with confident expectation of its fulfillment."

After sharing my testimony, I wrote a letter to Jan Crouch, Trinity Broadcasting Network (TBN), sharing my desire to help others going through similar experiences in life. I was going to mail the letter to Jan; however, I was heading to Coppell, Texas, to visit my son and his family the following weekend. I asked my son to find the address of TBN. While I was in the Dallas area, we drove to TBN headquarters in Irving, Texas. The beautiful white gate was open, and we drove through the gate and parked in the parking area. I prayed before entering the door on the side of the building for favor with Paul and Jan, but no one was around. I sat in a chair in the foyer by an office. I noticed a lady in the office diagonally across from where I was sitting, and I said hello. She walked out and proceeded to question me, and she stated she would be right back. Paul Crouch's brother, I believe his name was Phil, asked me how I got into TBN. I replied that the gate was open, and we drove through the opened gate and parked in the parking area. He said, "The gate was open?" I answered, "Yes, sir." He then asked how did I get into the building. I stated, "I just opened the door and walked in and sat down in a chair at the entrance area. Then, I approached the lady in the office and asked her if she could help me. She told me she would be right back, and now I am talking to you." He then asked how he could help me. I stated I had a letter for Jan Crouch and was wondering if I could give it to her or leave it for her to read. He stated she and Paul were not there; they were in California. However, he was flying to California the following morning, and he would be happy to hand-carry the letter to her. He took the letter and talked to me briefly. He stated that if God had allowed me in TBN, then he needed to get the letter to Paul and Jan. He proceeded to ask me if I minded answering why I was writing Jan. I explained I was drafting a manuscript and sharing my testimonies with her and how the Lord had given me a dream to write a letter and send it to Jan Crouch. Then, upon completion of writing the letter, He instructed me to take (hand carry) the letter to TBN in Irving, Texas. I did as the Lord instructed me, and God opened the gate/doors to TBN, and I was now standing in the TBN headquarters in Irving, Texas. I informed Phil what I had written in the letter. I shared with Jan I needed prayer regarding sharing my life journey. I penned a summary of the content of the manuscript in progress. Phil assured me he would give Jan the letter the following day when he arrived in California. Approximately two weeks later, I received a letter from Jan Crouch telling me thank you for the letter. And she was looking forward to reading my book when I got it published. She lovingly and caringly responded and encouraged me to complete the book because she felt it would help other women in an analogous situation. Her response is the reason I had the courage to move forward with the book. I felt honored she took the time to answer my letter. She was so gracious and stated she wanted to read my book upon completion and talk to me about the book at some point. She shared she would be praying for me. I am grateful for her kind gesture of love and thoughtfulness and for the gift of her time for me.

Needless to say, I was totally astonished that she responded to my letter. I did not get the book published due to a lack of funds. However, her words of encouragement that she would like to read the book kept me hoping to publish the book someday. Unfortunately, she passed away before I got the opportunity to publish the book. I am honored she read my letter and responded. Her letter gave me hope that publishing my book could become a reality someday. And that she was interested in reading it touched me deeply. We must remember that all things are possible through Christ. And that all things are in God's timing. We must never give up hope and have faith that all God instructs us to do will happen if we are obedient and trust Him.

CHAPTER FOUR

The Traumatic Journey:
"Betrayal of Mankind"

I believe that most people are abused in one way or another sometime during their lifetime. Some are abused verbally, while others are abused physically. Still, others may be wounded emotionally or dishonored sexually. Some may have experienced all forms of maltreatment. Abuse, traumatic circumstances, and betrayal have the same result: rejection. Other effects include shame, guilt, low self-esteem, despair, feeling unworthy, discouragement, controlled, loss of self-confidence, lack of inner peace, loss of self-respect, loss of hope, loss of identity ("who am I?"), loss of security, loss of freedom, leading to a life of total unhappiness and lack of purpose.

We may struggle with acceptance from others, and we may feel emotionally detached, but God created us for love and acceptance, and His plan is for us to have healthy and lasting relationships. John 10:10b (KJV): "I have come that they might have life, and that they might have it more abundantly."

> For God so loved the world [us] that He gave His one and only Son, that whoever believes in Him shall not perish but have everlasting life. For God did not send His Son into the world to condemn the world [us] but to save the world [us] through Him.
>
> John 3:16–17 (KJV)

We can believe in God and trust the love He gave us

through His only Son's death and that God rose Him from the dead. Hallelujah!

God revealed to me He did not send His Son to condemn me the week prior to sharing my testimony. He showed me it really did not matter what others thought of my life and that He loved me enough to give His one and only Son just for me. No one can ever love another more than the great sacrifice Jesus made for you and me. I had to believe what I had been taught by my precious mother. She was my spiritual rock and guide in God and Jesus Christ and through the power of the Holy Spirit. I honestly believe that her faithfulness in teaching me God's Word was the strength that sustained me through all of the abuse I endured. I had been immersed in the Word of God for many years, and I know without one doubt that this is the solitary thing that carried me through those traumatic events.

The Betrayals

My abuse never came from my family; it was from people I did not know or from acquaintances. The enemy will use people who are open to his deceitful ways and/or those who have been betrayed sometime in their lives. I was sexually, physically, verbally, mentally, emotionally, and spiritually abused from the time I can remember the first occurrence at the age of six until I remembered all the events that I had repressed deep in my heart. I was abused by several adult men in my childhood, and I had been rejected, traumatized, used, deceived, damaged emotionally, and betrayed.

I do not want to share all the details, but I will give a portion of my experiences, so you will believe I do know what it means to hurt and to share how I overcame and had victory. My reason for authoring this book is so others can understand that God absolutely loves each one of us and gives everyone hope through Jesus Christ. In sharing the experiences of my childhood, I have changed some of the names in order to protect the families of my perpetrators. Sometimes the word "perpetrator" will be used to maintain the dignity and privacy of others. I have no desire to hurt the innocent family members of my perpetrators. God has enabled me through His grace to say, "Father, forgive them, for they really did not know what they were doing" (Luke 23:34, KJV). I only reveal my story to give God and His precious Son, Jesus, all the glory for my life and healing and for the purpose of helping others who, like me, have been wounded and mistreated.

Mankind abused me several years ago. It all began when I was six years young. A neighbor's fourteen-year-old son molested me. My father had come home from work, and my mother told him I was missing, and she could not find me. They continued the search for me together. I heard his voice, and I said to my perpetrator, "That is my father looking for me; I have to go." He let me go and said if I told anyone what he had done to me that he would kill my dog and hurt me. That was my first experience of feeling fear and lack of "understanding" of what had happened that day. I was a happy child with a great sense of security from my parents, but this experience left me with great fear, so I honored his "threat" and told no one.

At the age of twelve, I was molested again. This time it was in my own front yard, by a person I knew. We lived in a small town where everyone knew each other. This man was in his early twenties at the time. He was the butcher in the meat department at our local grocery store. My mother was gone to the store (imagine that), and my two-year-old brother and I were home alone. We were playing in our front yard, and "my perpetrator" pulled into our driveway. He said hello and asked me to come to the car. I had no reason to mistrust him and, as a child, did what he asked. He then told me to get in the car because he wanted to talk to me. I complied. He began to touch me inappropriately. I got scared and felt this was not right. I told him to stop and kicked him. He let go of me, and I got out of the car. He got out and grabbed my arm and told me he would hurt my brother and take him away forever, and I would never see him again if I said anything. Anyway, he said no one would believe me, and I had better not tell anyone. This really scared me, so I told no one about this for twenty-eight years.

This was only the beginning of the enemy's strikes against me. He was tearing down the confidence I had in sharing with others about Jesus. I became afraid of people (adults) and started staying to myself. Therefore, the sharing of Jesus decreased. I became intimidated by others older than me and withdrawn. I did not trust people. Being a child, I did not have the biblical knowledge to fight this type of battle. Satan took advantage of this and began his all-out war against me. He knew God had a specific plan for my life.

Then, at the age of fourteen, I was raped by a twenty-eight-year-old man that lived one and one-half blocks from where I lived. He grabbed me one day while walking home from school and took me to an isolated area, held me at knifepoint, and tied me up. By God's grace, I fought with all my strength, kicking him, thus disabling him, and I managed to get away but not quite soon enough. Upon getting myself out of his control and bondage, I started walking toward town. I was terrified of the dark; I was cold, lonely, and scared. It was in late fall, and this became a time of the year I did not like. I was always sad during this season.

When I arrived home, I went straight to my room and pondered the events of what had happened to me. I was very naïve, felt something bad had happened, and I simply did not understand. When my father came to my room to check on me, I tried to explain to him why I was getting home so late from school and tried to clarify what had happened, but he just told me we would discuss it later. My father never confronted me in anger, as he was upset at my late arrival home. He would always discuss things when he was calm, thus telling me to go to sleep as it was extremely late, and we would discuss this tomorrow.

The following morning, my perpetrator/rapist/abuser caught me walking to school, and he strongly and emphatically told me he would kill me if I said a word to anyone regarding what had happened the previous evening. At this moment, the root of fear greatly impacted my life. Daily, before school and after school, he would drive by and yell at me, "If you say one word, you will not live. I will kill you!" Intimidation can be immensely powerful in a young person's life. Every time I walked to and from school, fear would overpower me. I was always glad when I would arrive home and enjoy the safety and privacy of my abode. This was the third event in my life that I kept buried. I was a freshman in high school at the time of this offense. I was a straight "A" student, and my grades plummeted to "Cs" and "Ds." In the last nine weeks of my freshman year, my grades began to improve. This event had a huge impact on my emotional and mental status. I felt so much shame, guilt, hurt, *fear*, confusion, and many other emotions, which caused my self-confidence to be shattered.

A few weeks after my devastating experience, this same man raped another girl in my school. "Kathy" told her parents, and when he found this out, he kidnapped her, beat her, and left her seriously injured. He had literally thrown her through his windshield. This really caused me to have an even greater fear of him. I emphatically realized he meant what he said. This taught me that it was not permissible to talk about what had happened and the many emotions I felt and still did not understand. I learned I had to stuff my feelings and never express them to anyone.

Kathy's parents pressed charges against this man, and when it went to court, justice did not prevail. It was amazing how many girls showed up at court to support her. Unfortunately, the perpetrator's family had a great deal of money, and the judge was paid off. This was common knowledge as this man had been "bought off" for many offenses he had done. I was thankful that I said nothing to anyone. Kathy came to school on several occasions battered and bruised as this man continually harassed her. She eventually made sure she was never alone; invariably, someone was with her.

I was thankful the company my father worked for transferred to another location. My life was peaceful for a couple of years. When I was sixteen years old, another traumatic event occurred. One Friday night, I was at a friend's house, and we were listening to music, having an enjoyable evening looking at TEEN Magazine. I left her house around 11:30 p.m. as I had to be home at midnight. As I was driving home, I was forced off the road by another vehicle. There were five guys in this vehicle, and they attacked me brutally. I was hit in the head with a heavy object making everything "fuzzy" after that point. I had been raped and beaten, and I could hear them laughing and saying all kinds of appalling and frightful things about me. (God revealed something to me regarding this incident later in my life when I shared my testimony. God had lifted my spirit above the violent attack on my body.) I heard them say, "She's dead; we better get out of here."

This event terrorized me repeatedly for about a year. Every time I would drive somewhere alone, I was always looking in my mirrors to make sure no one was following me. Every corner I turned, I was suspicious of others. If a car passed me, I would either speed up to prevent passage or slow down and let them move ahead of me. I would feel great apprehension if I were boxed in by several vehicles. I was always very observant of my surroundings. Second Timothy 1:7 (KJV), "For

God hath not given me a spirit of fear; but of power, and of love, and of a sound mind." This scripture became a particularly important part of my life.

However, I did tell my mom about this incident, and she called our family doctor, and the doctor came to our home to check on me. This was when doctors made house calls. He checked me over and stated I had a severe concussion but no broken bones. He told my mother that he had never seen anyone so maliciously beaten. Our doctor was a close family friend of my grandparents. The doctor telephoned his cousin, who worked for the sheriff's department, and asked him to talk to my mom and me the following day. I could not identify the guys. I did not know them, nor could I describe the vehicle they were driving. I did not know their tag number due to the fact they came up behind me, and I could not see that well at night. Thus, making it difficult or almost impossible to find them. They were never found. I eventually buried this event so deeply that I did not remember it until I was in therapy twenty-plus years later. I literally locked these events in my heart and put a prison wall with a padlocked door around my mind and heart. I took the key and threw it as far as I could because the memories of these events were too painful to remember. I thought there was something wrong with me. Why were these people so mean and ruthless to me? What did I do to deserve this treatment?

Questions regarding feelings of maltreatment:

Have you ever been violated by someone?

_____

_____

_____

_____

As you remember this violation, how did you feel at that moment? Sad, angry, hurt, pain, sense of loss, confused, alone, dirty, used, attacked, worthless, and/or damaged?

_____

_____

_____

_____

I can remember the day that I pulled this incident to the forefront of my mind. I was calm when telling my therapist this story. It was as if I was telling a story about another person. She encouraged me to stay the night with my daughter, who lived close by, because she was concerned this would "affect me in a few hours." She did not want me to take the long drive home alone. I went to my daughters for two or three hours and felt fine, so I decided to drive home. When I had driven approximately halfway home, the event I remembered earlier that day was revealed to the forefront of my mind and thoughts. Fear overcame me, and I do not remember driving the rest of the way home. It was as if I had blacked out. I know God helped me arrive home safely that night.

The next day my therapist called me to check on me. I was definitely not myself and was feeling lonely, depressed, and insecure. I had anxiety and fear, and I felt isolated and violated. This was difficult to face as these events began surfacing. I just wanted to stay in the house and not go to class. I was in college at the time. I had gone back to college when my children began college.

My instructors at college were incredibly supportive during this period of my life. I wanted to quit college and was at the point where I did not know how I could concentrate well enough to study and pass my exams. My focus was misplaced at the moment. Every one of my instructors refused to let me drop my classes and was very encouraging and willing to help me through this time of disarray. I was honest with them and let them know some of the emotions I was experiencing. They were understanding, sympathetic, and great encouragers, and none were judgmental.

My piano instructor, Dr. James Breckenridge, was a pillar of strength for me during this season of my life. He assigned music that was therapeutic and resulted in enhancing my stability, thus helping me to express my inner feelings. I gave my therapist permission to discuss my case with him. They worked together to help me deal successfully with the difficulties I was facing. I spent many piano lessons with tears streaming down my face, and Dr. Breckenridge was so caring and patient during my recovery process. The scripture Psalm 126:5 (KJV) came to mind, "They who sow in tears shall reap in joy!" I could relate to this scripture as I worked through the emotional pain. The many tears I shed were a great release and purging that eventually gave me joy and comfort. Tears are healing and help with the restoration of hurt, pain, and suffering. As I felt these painful emotions and released them, it produced a positive result; I could experience true joy instead of feeling affectedly mournful and cease camouflaging happiness and fake smiles.

I was working on my bachelor of arts in piano performance. Music provided a significant release of my inner emotions. I was required to practice eight hours a day for my graduate recital performance. Dr. Breckenridge gave me access to practice on the Steinway piano in his office, which allowed me privacy and the ability to focus without interruptions.

He thought it would be beneficial for me to enter collegiate-level competitions; however, opportunities were limited if one was over thirty years of age. He researched events compatible with my age range (forty-two), locating a competition I was qualified to enter. He recorded my performance of a Beethoven Sonata I was working on for my recital and entered it in an international audition. Eighteen pianists would be selected from twenty-six countries to perform in Graz, Austria. I was one of eighteen pianists chosen to perform in 1990 and 1992. I could not believe it. This event had an astounding effect on my self-confidence. God knew what He was doing by giving me a talent and the gift of expression of music through the voice of the piano. I still enjoy playing and find peace and comfort through the modality of music. I do not play classical music very much anymore; I express worship and praise to God through hymns and contemporary and sacred music.

The day arrived to travel to Austria, and my mother accompanied me. We were in Austria for two weeks and then spent twenty-one days touring Switzerland, Germany, France, England, Czechoslovakia, and Hungary. This was one of the most treasured highlights of my life experiences. I was beginning to believe in myself again. God has blessed me with many friends abroad, and I am so thankful that I had a wonderful professor in music who believed in me and encouraged me to do more than I ever dreamed possible. I always had a childhood dream of performing classical music, and God graciously gave me this opportunity to fulfill one of my life's desires.

Dr. Breckenridge took great interest in all his students. He passed away on March 27, 2009, and he will be greatly missed by all who knew him. I will always treasure the friendship we shared. We stayed close friends after I graduated from college, and I feel blessed to have found such a great friend and mentor. It is important to have someone in your life who can be a mentor, friend, or someone who is trustworthy and can keep confidentiality.

My therapist drove a long distance for my graduate recital, and that was special to me. She provided guidance and encouragement by helping me process the traumatic experiences in my life as well as giving me a foundation to cope with all that surfaced. God has placed many people in my life to encourage me and support me through my life's journey. I am richly blessed to have had so many stand beside me through the journey of healing from the many betrayals in my life.

I now understand the meaning of the words in the Bible stating that God does turn the bad around for good. How could good ever come from this abuse, betrayal, trauma, and evil done to me? God promises to take all things, even evil things, and turn them around for good in Romans 8:28. Think of these biblical examples: suffering causes you to commit your heart and soul to God. First Peter 4:19 (NIV): "So then, those who suffer according to God's will should commit themselves to their faithful Creator and continue to do good." Zondervan's commentary states, "God created the world, and he has faithfully ordered it and kept it since the creation. Because we know that God is faithful, we can count on him to fulfill his promises to us. If God can oversee the forces of nature, surely, he can see us through the trials we face."

I want to honor God with righteous behavior. I do not want to extol evil for evil. I want to do what God emulates and change all the evil around for good. And Hebrews 5:7 (NIV) states, "During the days of Jesus' life on earth, he offered up prayers and petitions with loud cries and tears to the one who could save him from death, and he was heard because of his reverent submission." Zondervan's commentary states, "Jesus was in great agony as he prepared to face death (Luke 22:41–44, NIV). Although Jesus cried out to God, asking to be delivered, He was prepared to suffer humiliation, separation from His Father, and death in order to do God's will. At times we will undergo trials, not because we want to suffer, but because we want to obey God. Let Jesus' obedience sustain and encourage you in times of trial. You will be able to face anything if you know that Jesus Christ is with you.

I believe the abuse I endured was allowed so God could use the strength He gave me to help others who have been abused. All He requires of me is to be obedient to Him, come to Him in prayer, and yield myself to Him. As God set me free, He took the evil inflicted on me and turned it around for good. He did this by allowing me the opportunity to share with others the insight and wisdom He has given me. Praise be to the God and Father of our Lord Jesus Christ, the Father of compassion and the God of all comfort, who comforts us in all our troubles so that we can comfort those in any trouble with the comfort we ourselves have received from God. Freedom and victory are gifts. We can overcome the betrayal of mankind and experience freedom and victory in our lives. "Be still before the Lord and wait patiently for Him; do not fret when men succeed in their ways when they carry out their wicked schemes" (Psalm 37:7, NIV). "The Lord replied, My Presence will go with you, and I will give you rest" (Exodus 33:14, Zondervan's Life Application Bible).

CHAPTER FIVE

The Journey of Dereliction: "Spousal Abuse"

My experience with spousal abuse was very devastating. Spousal abuse is the state of being abandoned by another and the failure of another to fulfill their obligation. In the beginning, our marriage was strong, we were happy, and I thought our marriage was as sound as any marriage could be. We were introduced to each other through a mutual friend, and we dated for two years, took a break from each other for three years, got back together, and were married two months later. During our high school years, we attended the same church. After we were married, we continued attending our home church until we moved to Kansas. We had two beautiful children, a thirteen-room home, and two automobiles and were involved in church, and everything was going well.

After moving to Kansas, we were still incredibly involved in church and the community. My husband was an elder at church, and he drove the church/Sunday school bus every Sunday. We were youth leaders and Sunday school teachers and held many leadership positions in the church. I was the church pianist and sometimes played the organ for services. He had a passion for God and helping others with a great appreciation for all that God had done for us. God always blessed our family, and if anyone had told me how drastically our lives would change, I would not have believed them.

We acquired a business in another town and relocated. This was when our lives began to change. My husband became friends with other business owners in the community. One of the men who owned a business across the street from ours lost everything and ended up taking his own life. My husband was the person who found him. His friend had shot himself in the mouth with a 410 shotgun. After this incident, he did not cope with this memory very well. Every time he would lie down to go to sleep, he would see his business colleague the way he found him. He would drink to try and wipe out this memory. He began to miss church periodically and started making choices that did not reflect his character. His decision to drink led him down an unhealthy path. Approximately a year later, he was drinking heavily on a daily basis. He slowly became addicted to alcohol, thus becoming an alcoholic. Along with the drinking, his personality took a 180-degree turn. His addiction to alcohol turned him into a man I did not recognize. He did not realize the doors he was opening through the choices he was making, thus reaping the consequences of his addiction.

Our pastor talked to him on several occasions but with no avail. My husband would not give up the alcohol and was blinded by the decisions he was making. The more he drank, the more violent he became and the more his thinking became altered. Alcohol is considered a mind-altering drug, and it causes deprivation of the mind. He was living in a vicious cycle that impacted not only his life but my life and our children's lives. Our choices will follow us throughout life to our final destiny. We must take accountability for the choices we make. That is why we need to do as Paul did and die daily to ourselves. We must have the mind of Christ to be able to make the right choices in life.

The first time my husband beat me, I cowered down in the corner of the living room, crying and asking him what was wrong with him. He told me to shut up and called me horrible names as he continued beating me. I curled up in a fetal position trying to protect myself. I was in a state of shock for several hours, not understanding what was going on with the man I had married. Who was this person, and what happened to him? The beatings became more and more frequent. He began to accuse me of having affairs with different men. He told me I was fat and ugly, I was a church freak, and many other horrible things too numerous to mention. He blamed God for everything. It was as if he had developed two personalities. I felt like I was living with "Dr. Jekyll and Mr. Hyde." He became jealous of my activities at church; however, everyone was supportive of the children and me. They even apologized for his behavior and asked what they could do to help. I did not know what to say except, "Please, pray for him." I came home from church one Sunday night, and he pointed a gun at me and said he would kill me if I went back to church. I told him I was not going to quit going to church. My pastor talked to me and told me I needed to take my children to a safe place and leave before he succeeded and killed me. We lived in Kansas, and our families lived in Oklahoma. The threats became more intense, and he started yelling at the children. I talked with my pastor and thought maybe the best thing to do was go to Oklahoma, hoping a separation would help him look at himself. I told my husband I was going to take our children and go to Oklahoma for the summer and give him time to think about what he wanted to do with his life. That is when he told me he wanted a divorce because he was involved with another woman. I was devastated. I told him I did not want a divorce; I wanted him to be his old self and come back to church with our children and me. He said no and told me to leave.

That night while I was sleeping, he came home in a drunken stupor and woke me up with a gun pointed at the side of my head. He beat me, and I knew he was going to kill me if I did not leave. The next morning, I called my pastor and told him I was leaving immediately. He called the men from the church, and they brought a U-Haul truck and loaded all my furniture and belongings.

They gave me money to cover expenses for the trip to Oklahoma and enough to rent a house and pay for the first couple of months' utilities and household expenses. I rented a house, found a job, and after getting settled, I realized how my life had changed over the past couple of years. I had forgotten how nice it was to have a peaceful night's sleep. My mother and mother-in-law helped with the children, and things were beginning to settle down for us. I continued to pray for my husband and asked God to reveal to him how much he was losing and to think about where he would go if Jesus broke the eastern sky.

A couple of months passed, and I received a phone call from my husband; he said he was sorry and wanted to come to Oklahoma to be with his family. I told him I would not tolerate his drinking and that if this was what he really wanted, he would have to make better choices. He would have to work on straightening his life out and getting right with God. He said he was willing to do all the above and said he would even go to counseling. I felt as though God was answering my prayers. I wanted my family back. He sold our business and arrived in Oklahoma within two weeks of our conversation. He moved in with us and acquired work. Everything was going well.

He decided he wanted to get back into farming and rented pasture and farm ground. We bought several heads of cattle, and our lives were taking a turn upward. He was attending church with the children and me, and everything was good again.

Approximately one year later, I came home from work, and he was drinking. My heart was grievously heavy when I saw this. He said he had been drinking for a couple of months and laughed about it. It did not take long, and he was drinking even more than ever, and the abuse became unbearable. I had bruises all over me, and this was humbling, embarrassing, and humiliating. I worked for an oil company as an assistant office manager and was providing a living for my children. My boss was incredibly supportive and understanding. He asked me why I tolerated this behavior and suggested I get a divorce. I told him I did not believe in divorce; therefore, I felt I was going to have to endure the current situation to keep my family together.

On September 5, the company I worked for was having a meeting with all the employees. The president of the company came for the meeting from Houston. The night before (September 4), my husband came home drunk and beat me severely. He hit me between the eyes, causing an open wound injury. My children ran to my best friend's (GG's) and told her what had happened. She immediately came to the house. Upon arrival, she had me hold a towel and ice on the wound, applying pressure to help stop the bleeding. She proceeded to drive me to the hospital emergency room. The doctor did not want to close the wound with stitches because he said it would leave a terrible scar on my face/forehead. He butterflied the wound. His method worked, and I only have a hairline scar where this injury was inflicted. My husband came to the hospital and was abusive to me and threatened the doctor. The hospital staff called the sheriff, and he arrested my husband. My children were terrified of their father after this incident. I went to work the following morning, September 5, and my boss could not believe I had come to work so beaten. He told me I could not continue to live like this. The president of the company talked to me and asked if there was anything they could do to help in my situation. He offered to let me transfer to Houston, Texas, but I did not want to take my children away from their grandparents and school. I opted to stay and keep my family together. I asked my husband to please go with me for counseling. He refused. I continued praying for him. It seemed the more I prayed, the worse he would get. I did not understand why God was not answering my prayers. I talked to my pastor and told him I prayed for my husband many hours every day. He said, "Marylin, God will not make him stop drinking. He gave everyone free will. God would not force him to make the right choices." My pastor told me that God had given me two beautiful children, and it was my responsibility to keep them safe since my husband would not be responsible and provide a safe environment for our family. He told me I needed to leave before he killed me. He asked me what my children would do if my husband succeeded in killing me. I said I did not know. He told me to think and pray about that and to get back to him with my thoughts regarding this.

The beatings progressively worsened, and I was in and out of the emergency room quite frequently. One beating was so bad that I was transferred to a hospital forty-five miles from where we lived, and I was unconscious for three days. I had police protection by my door for the duration of my hospital stay. I knew if something was not done soon, I would be dead. I could not, in my own conscience, justify bringing myself to leave him and get a divorce. This went against everything I was taught; you stay in your marriage and make it work. I knew in my heart it takes two to make a marriage work. One cannot do it alone. Actually, it takes more for a marriage to work: God, Christ, husband, and wife.

I did finally convince him to go to counseling. We went to a doctor (psychiatrist) in a nearby city, and my husband accused me of having an affair with the doctor. My husband felt as though the doctor was siding with me. My husband refused to go after the second session. I started going to another counselor, a woman, so I would not be accused of having an affair. Suddenly, his excuse was she was a female and females stuck together. According to my husband, no matter what I did, it was never the right decision made. This counselor advised me to get out of this situation before I was killed. She told me that he would continue to get worse and succeed in killing me. I needed to protect myself and my children, and she said living in this situation was not healthy for my children. I knew this in my heart, but I felt I was going against God if I left. I was taught that you keep the family together no matter what happens.

The physical, sexual, verbal, and emotional abuse never stopped. I was not getting any sleep because he would keep me up all night. I was at the point of exhaustion and did not know what to do. I would call the sheriff, and he would come to arrest him and hold him for twenty-four hours, and the kids and I would have peace for that duration of time. Then, he would get out of jail and get drunk, and the abuse would start all over again. It was a vicious cycle that seemed to never end.

An example of how he was getting worse is he came to church and pointed a gun at me while I was playing the piano and grabbed me by the arm, and forced me out of the church. My friend, GG, took my children home and called the sheriff. The sheriff said, "Marylin, you cannot keep living like this. He is going to kill you, and he is getting progressively worse." The sheriff told me he had had enough of his maniacal behavior, and something had to be done.

My husband's mother, brother, and I went to court and persuaded him to be admitted for twenty-eight days to have him dried out and for counseling and observation. After twenty-eight days, he was released, and he did well for about two weeks; then, he fell back into his addiction and abusive behavior. I could not take anymore and left him and moved about thirty miles away so I could keep my job and have the means to take care of my children. The humiliation and embarrassment were becoming more than we could bear.

The separation did not stop the abuse. He would break into our home and continue to beat me, call me names, and accuse me of the most horrible things. I always had neighbors that would take my children when he would beat me. My son would lie in his bed and literally shake from fear every night. I would hold him in my arms, and he would cry and say, "Is Daddy going to hurt you again, Mommy?" I told him not to worry; we would be okay and went to sleep. Jesus would keep us safe. I would tightly hold him in my arms until he fell asleep. Then, he would be awakened during the night by the crushing sound of his father breaking down the door or coming through a window. My daughter, age twelve at the time, appeared to be the stronger child and not so terrified of him. She was two years older than her brother, but she did not appear to be as shaken as much during the abusive years as her brother. My son had developed a spirit of fear. She would get her brother and go to a neighbor's and call the sheriff to get help. Our family was on a first-name basis with the sheriff. Michelle had his number memorized and said, "Richard, Dad is here again." He would always be at the house within five to ten minutes.

My son asked me why we did not move far away from where his dad could never find us. My daughter asked me why I did not divorce him, and I said because I did not believe in divorce, and I was continuing to pray that he would stop drinking. My prayers were never answered, not because of God but because my husband chose not to do what was right. The abuse continued as he became more desperate to control me. He started coming to my job, and my boss would lock me in the linen closet, so he could not get to me until the sheriff would get there to arrest him. My boss called me into the office one morning, and I thought I was getting a pink slip because my husband was interfering with my job. He would call every five minutes, harassing me. But thankfully, God protected me and my job, as I did not get a pink slip. I had to support myself and my children. My boss asked me, "What are your children going to do if this man succeeds and kills you?" I said I do not know. He also asked, "What would you do if, in trying to kill you, he kills one of your children?" I told him I could not live with that scenario. I would never forgive myself. He then said he had something to share with me. He had a sister who lived in a similar situation as me. Her husband would abuse her, she would have him arrested, he would be in jail twenty-four hours, and then he would get out, and the cycle would never end. One night, he almost succeeded in killing her. She was hospitalized for two weeks, and she finally pressed charges against him for attempted murder. He ended up hanging himself in his cell, and she could not forgive herself for pressing charges against him.

He then told me he had called the president of the company, and they agreed to give me three weeks' leave of absence with pay. Arrangements were made for my children to be out of school for three weeks, and an itinerary of their assignments and homework for them to complete so they would not fall behind. The men who worked for the company I worked for collected money and put new tires on my car, changed the oil, and had my car tuned up that morning.

The company I worked for sent my children and me to Disneyland and to other places for a three-week vacation with all expenses paid. My boss had a brother who was in law enforcement, and he made arrangements to have official law enforcement escort us to California. My boss told me to get some rest and clear my head and think about the two questions he had asked me. I needed to make a decision, and he said I needed to get a divorce and put a stop to all this madness. I promised I would give this some serious thought.

My pastor told me before we left on the trip that God understood my situation and to think about the fact that I had two children to protect. He said the abuse would never stop, and I did not have a choice. I had to get away from this person.

In most cases, when the wife divorces the man, the abuse will eventually stop.

After we returned from California, I made the decision to get a divorce. I did not have the money to get a divorce, but through others' concern for my life and my children's lives, the money was provided. So many people were tired of my husband harassing me and beating me. I took the advice of my counselor, pastor, boss, and others, and I filed for a divorce.

Sometime after I filed, the kids and I went to visit my mom one weekend. We left Friday when they got out of school. We came home on Sunday at about 1:30 a.m., and we walked into a huge nightmare. My husband had broken into the house, smashed all my dishes except one plate, demolished my furniture, sliced the mattress on my bed with a butcher knife, and left the knife stuck in the mattress, ripped all my clothes into shreds, cut all my shoes up with a razor blade, tore every page out of the phone book, and wrote on the pages with a magic marker, "I will kill you b...." Then, he nailed the pages on the walls of every room in the house. I was terrified and called the sheriff. I told him he would not believe what had been done to my house. While on the phone with the sheriff, I heard my husband pull into the driveway. I told the kids to get in the car because I could get away from him more easily if I did not have to worry about getting them out of the house. They went to the car, and my husband came into the house carrying a twenty-two rifle. He said he was going to kill me. I got away from him and ran to my car. My son was not there. I asked my daughter, "Where is your brother?" She said he had gone back into the house through the back door. I yelled for him to get in the car. In my heart and thoughts, I had had enough of his father's maniacal behavior; I could not take anymore. About that time, my son came running around the corner of the house to the car, his father shot the rifle, and the bullet missed my son by about two inches. At that moment, I snapped. I told my son to get on the floorboard of the front passenger seat, and my daughter was in the back seat, and I told her to get down. I backed my 1978 Camaro up into the street and pushed the accelerator all the way to the floor, and tried to run over him. At that instant, I was going to kill him. He almost shot my son. He ran toward his Corvette, and I was going toward him at full speed. He jumped over his car, and I slammed into the side of his Corvette as he was jumping over his car.

The sheriff pulled up as my husband was jumping over his car. He grabbed him, slapped handcuffs on him, put him in the back of the sheriff's car, and got his rifle and gave it to me. Then he asked me what had happened, and he also talked to my neighbor Lois. My neighbor explained to the sheriff what had transpired. After he heard the details, he said, "Too bad I didn't hit him." He stated he was so tired of his behavior and abuse. He assessed the damage to his Corvette and said, "I did major damage to his car." Then he looked at my Camaro and said, "I do not believe it; there is no damage to your vehicle. There is not even a scratch on your car!" If it was not for the damage to his Corvette, the sheriff said one would think I did not hit his car. (The insurance denied the claim to repair his Corvette because I damaged it, and it was still in both our names. So, they would not pay for damage done to our own property because my name was also on the title at this time.) My husband was furious about the damage to his vehicle and was going to sue me to replace his vehicle because the insurance did not cover the damage. Upon the insurance assessment regarding the 1978 Camaro, there was not even a scratch on my vehicle. It totaled his Corvette. Needless to say, he was livid about his vehicle but with no remorse about the fear he instilled in his son, daughter, and me. He had not one word to say regarding shooting toward our child and just missing him and almost hitting him with the bullet that was intended for me.

The sheriff said, "Marylin, I am going to make a recommendation for you and the kids to be entered into a police safeguard/protection program." We left the area and lived hidden and undercover for several months. I still had my job with the Oil Company, and my children went to the same school. The sheriff had someone from the sheriff's department follow me to work to make sure we arrived safely. My boss's wife would take my children to school with an escort from the sheriff's department.

After the divorce was final, I felt worthless, as if I were in darkness and I had committed the worse sin ever. I had so much guilt and unforgiveness toward myself for a long time. Someone had anonymously mailed me a book by Billy Graham titled *Peace with God*. This book helped me realize I was not a bad person for getting a divorce. It helped me to forgive myself and gave me back my life. Powerful book!

It has been almost forty years since my divorce, and my children's father has not changed. I still pray for him that he will come to the realization that his life needs to be transformed by the renewing of his mind, and he needs deliverance from the life he has chosen before it is too late. He is about six feet tall and weighs eighty-two pounds. The alcohol has destroyed his life. He has been committed so many times to dry out with no permanent change in his life. I have visited him many times when he has been institutionalized. It breaks my heart to see how he has allowed Satan to destroy his life.

One time, my daughter called me and asked me to go with her to see him when he was being dried out, and I agreed to go. I sat on the edge of the bed and asked him if I could pray for him. He said yes, but he wanted to ask me a question first. The question was, "How can you always have a smile on your face? I never see you that you do not smile." I told him that was easy. It is because Jesus was in my heart, and I have great joy because He loves me so much. I sang a song to him that I taught my children when they were small. The words are:

Happy, happy, happy, happy, happy;

Happy are the people whose God is the Lord;

Happy, happy, happy, happy, happy,

Happy are the people whose God is the Lord.

Now, where does this happy feeling come from—Jesus;

Where does this happy feeling come from?

This happy feeling comes from Jesus every day,

He more than pleases, and that's where this happy feeling comes from.

Tears began to roll down his cheeks, and he said he had done so many bad things that Jesus could never love him again. I told him, yes, He can and does! For a moment, I thought he was going to allow Jesus to set him free from the bondage he was in and allow Jesus to give him peace. But, when he was released from rehab, he went back to his weakness, and the alcohol took over his life again. He continues making wrong choices to this day. I will never give up on him until he takes his last breath. He has emphysema and alcohol dementia, and the doctors have said he should be dead, but I believe God keeps giving him another day to change his life.

We must love and forgive those who hurt us. They are in

worse pain than we are. God has given me compassion, peace, and forgiveness for all those who have abused me. My prayer is that all my abusers and perpetrators will know Christ before it is too late. That is why the Jesus I know died. He died for the brokenhearted, He died for those in bondage, He died to set the captives free, and we can never give up on them. They are hurting, desperate people who need our prayers, compassion, love, and forgiveness. Remember what Jesus said on the cross, "Father forgive them for they know not what they do" (Luke 23:34, KJV). We need to intercede for all who are wounded. God tells us in Matthew 25:35–36,

> For I was hungry, and you gave me something to eat, I was thirsty and you gave me something to drink, I was a stranger and you invited me in, I needed clothes and you clothed me, I was sick and you looked after me, I was in prison and you came to visit me.
>
> Matthew 25:35–36 (NIV)

Alcoholism is a sickness, a choice, and a sin. People who are hurting are hungry for something or someone to fill the void. This emptiness can only be filled with God's love, mercy, grace, kindness, and forgiveness. As for my children's father, he was not in prison, but he was in bondage and was imprisoned in his alcohol addiction. He needs to believe God loves him and that he has a way of being set free. In God's Word, we are given hope for those who are in bondage and captivity.

> The Spirit of the Lord is on me, because he has anointed me to preach good news to the poor, He has sent me to proclaim freedom for the prisoners and recovery of sight for the blind, to release the oppressed, to proclaim the year of the Lord's favor.
>
> Luke 4:18–19 (NIV)

The Spirit of the Lord is on me, because the Lord has anointed me to preach good news to the poor. He has sent me to bind up the brokenhearted, to proclaim freedom for the captives, and release from darkness for the prisoners, to proclaim the year of the Lord's favor.

Isaiah 61:1–2a (NIV)

Sometimes, we are prisoners in our own minds and hearts. We need to help those who are in bondage by interceding for them. Pray for the release of the bondage and proclaim victory over what the enemy has done to their lives. Job 33:14–30 is my prayer for my children's father,

> For God does speak, now one way, now another, though man may not perceive it in a dream, in a vision of the night, when deep sleep falls on men as they slumber in their beds, he may speak in their ears and terrify them with warnings, to turn man from wrongdoing and keep him from pride, to preserve his soul from the pit, his life from perishing by the sword. Or a man may be chastened on a bed of pain with constant distress in his bones, so that his very being finds food repulsive and his soul loathes the choicest meal. His flesh wastes away to nothing, and his bones, once hidden, now stick out. His soul draws near to the pit, and his life to the messengers of death. Yet if there is an angel on his side as a mediator, one out of a thousand, to tell a man what is right for him, to be gracious to him and say, Spare him from going down to the pit, I have found a ransom for him—then his flesh is renewed like a child's; it is restored as in the days of his youth. He prays to God and finds favor with him, he sees God's face and shouts for joy; he is restored by God to his righteous state. Then he comes to men and says, I sinned, and perverted what was right, but I

did not get what I deserved. He redeemed my soul from going down to the pit, and I will live to enjoy the light. God does all these things to a man—twice, even three times—to turn back his soul from the pit, that the light of life may shine on him.

Job 33:14–30 (NIV)

To me, praying this scripture in Job is for our lost loved ones and trusting that God can reveal Himself to them and save them from the pit.

"What Is 'Spousal Abuse'?" Jelena Woehr, eHow contributing writer, states the following,

> "Spousal abuse" is any type of physical, sexual, or psychological violence within a marriage. When spousal abuse involves physical violence, it is also referred to as domestic violence. Every type of spousal abuse is a serious crime. No person should have to live in fear of their spouse. Spousal abuse comes in many forms. Physical abuse occurs when a spouse is physically violent toward a partner. Verbal abuse is characterized using words to dominate and humiliate a partner. Emotional abuse is similar to verbal abuse but encompasses a wider range of actions. An emotionally abusive spouse is likely verbally abusive also but will use other psychological tactics to control the victim. Sexual abuse is the act of forcing someone to participate in any sexual act or situation against their will. Many victims of physical abuse are also subjected to sexual abuse. Financial abuse is the use of money to dominate and control a partner. There are many misconceptions regarding spousal abuse. Although awareness of spousal abuse has increased in recent years, many people still cling to misconceptions about what spousal abuse is,

who can be a victim, and what motivates abusers. It is often assumed that only men abuse their spouses and only women are victims of spousal abuse. Abuse can happen in any relationship. Another common misconception is that abusers "lose control" when they harm their victims. Yet, most abusers are capable of delaying or intentionally hiding abuse, which requires choice and premeditation. Abuse results from a conscious choice made by the abuser.

Warning Signs

The warning signs of spousal abuse are often present in the earliest stages of a relationship. Jealous and controlling behavior is one warning sign of abuse. (On a personal note: other "red flags" are road rage, expression of anger over insignificant things, and one who is cruel to animals. A person who is rebellious toward authority figures, God, church, and others.) Another warning sign is the inability to accept blame. The abuser will say, "You made me angry," not "I was angry." This can easily become, "You made me hit you." Sudden mood swings are also characteristic of a potential abuser. The abuser may be laughing, saying nice things, being calm one moment, and making threats of violence the next. These threats will then be dismissed by the abuser saying, "Oh, I was just kidding." "I didn't mean it." "Seriously, I was joking." "I promise I won't do it again!"

Patterns of Abuse

Most abusers follow a clearly defined pattern of thinking and behavior called the cycle of violence. First, the abuser harms the victim. This abuse is intended to control and dominate the victim. Next, the abuser feels guilty. This concern focuses more on the risk of getting caught than on the victim's well-being. The abuser will apologize and promise never to harm the abused partner again. For a period of time, the abuser will behave normally. This "honeymoon period" may convince the victim to stay in an abusive relationship, believing that the abuser really has changed for good. Soon the abuser will begin planning and fantasizing about how to abuse the victim next. The abuser dwells on past resentments that he perceives as justifiable actions by the victim that needs to be corrected or controlled. Finally, the abuser sets the victim up for abuse by creating a situation in which the victim cannot meet the abuser's unrealistic expectations; thus, the abuser feels justified in harming the victim, and the cycle begins again. If you are a victim of spousal abuse, you need to escape to a safe place. Dial 911 for help or call the National Domestic Violence Hotline at 1-800-799-7233 from a safe location where your partner cannot discover you seeking help and react with violence. In most areas, shelters and other assistance are available to people escaping abusive relationships. Children and pets may also be victims of abuse in a household where a spouse is abused. You can obtain help for children through child services, and for pets, there are animal rescue programs that are available to provide temporary shelter. The most important factor is to get help!

Police/sheriff departments can ensure that the abused partner, children, and pets in the home can be removed safely and placed where they can be safe and receive care and counseling. Also, the victim can press charges, and the abuser can be arrested. This will give the victim time to find a safe place before the abuser is released.

The abuser needs counseling to recover from the need to control his life. The victim also needs counseling to help in dealing with the stress and damage done to the victim physically, emotionally, sexually, and mentally. There are many options available to help the abuser and the victims. Marriage counseling is definitely a great option. Seek help through your pastor, Christian therapist, or biblical counselor. Most importantly, trust God to help you through a difficult time. God will give you the strength to endure the pain and suffering. Lean on Him and know that you are important to Him. He loves you and does not want His precious children treated brutally. You are special to Him, you are His child, and you are worthy to be loved and accepted. He will carry you through the bad and the ugly. He will give you guidance through the Holy Spirit. He will keep you in His arms. The Lord knows your name and what you are going through. He is there for you; all you have to do is let Him surround you with His love and compassion. He gave His Son, Jesus, so you could be set free. He does not want you to be a slave or in bondage to abuse or to live in fear.

Me, my son, and my daughter.

I am truly blessed. I prayed over my children and asked God to protect their hearts and minds. I asked God to help them come out of this unscathed and without emotional damage. God answered my prayers. We serve an awesome God. I am so thankful for the many blessings he has bestowed upon me. I have two wonderful children, a devoted, loving son, and a very precious, loving, and devoted daughter. I am truly blessed with a wonderful son-in-law and daughter-in-law and nine beautiful grandchildren, and six great-grandchildren.

Family picture.

My children's father passed away on June 16, 2019. He was in a nursing home at the time of his death. He was not drinking while in the nursing home. He did ask for forgiveness for his choices in life. I can share that he told me he was sorry for all he put our children and me through; I did tell him that I forgave him and that Jesus forgives him, also. I feel in my spirit he did ask for forgiveness from God because he made an effort to ask for forgiveness for the wrongs he had done in life regarding those he hurt. However, only God and His Son, Jesus, know the true answer to that question. We serve a God of mercy and grace, and Jesus died so we can all be forgiven. I believe in my heart he made the choice and asked God for forgiveness. His countenance was changed the last time I talked to him. He is at peace now and healed from his sickness/addiction.

I am so thankful for what Jesus did for all who are hurting and in pain. Jesus is the way, the truth, and the life. Jesus is the true answer for those who are hurting, and everyone in the world today is in need of a Savior, Redeemer, and Healer, and only Jesus can embrace each and every person and bring us to complete restoration.

Domestic Violence Statistics by State

As stated in the article "State-by-State Statistics on Domestic Violence," Domestic violence is a violence or abuse in a domestic setting, such as in cohabitation or marriage. Domestic violence is often used as a synonym for intimate partner violence, which involves a spouse or intimate partner in an intimate partner relationship.

Domestic violence can happen to anyone of any age and can occur in both heterosexual and same-sex relationships. Domestic violence can also include violence against children, parents, or the elderly and can take on several forms, including physical, verbal, emotional, and sexual abuse.

The abuser often believes that the abuse is an entitlement, acceptable, justified, or unlikely to be reported. Victims often feel trapped by the abuser in domestic violence situations through isolation by their abuser from family and friends, lack of finances, fear, shame, cultural acceptance, and power and control. Victims can develop physical disabilities and chronic health problems as well as severe psychological disorders.

State	Against Women ▼
Oklahoma	49.10%
Iowa	45.30%
Kentucky	45.30%
North Carolina	43.90%
Nevada	43.80%
Alaska	43.30%
Arizona	42.60%
Washington	42.60%
Idaho	42.50%
Missouri	41.70%
Hawaii	41.50%
South Carolina	41.50%
Arkansas	40.80%
Tennessee	40.00%
Mississippi	39.70%
Maine	39.30%

Connecticut	37.70%
Pennsylvania	37.70%
Delaware	37.60%
Alabama	37.50%
Florida	37.40%
Oregon	37.30%
Montana	37.20%
Utah	36.90%
Colorado	36.80%
Michigan	36.10%
Kansas	35.90%
Louisiana	35.90%
New Jersey	35.80%
Wyoming	35.80%
Ohio	35.60%
Illinois	35.30%
California	34.90%
New Hampshire	34.70%

Texas	34.50%
Maryland	34.40%
New Mexico	34.40%
Indiana	33.90%
Massachusetts	33.90%
Minnesota	33.90%
Nebraska	33.70%
South Dakota	33.70%
Vermont	33.60%
West Virginia	33.60%
Georgia	33.00%
Wisconsin	32.40%
New York	31.70%
Virginia	31.30%
Rhode Island	29.90%
North Dakota	25.30%

As the statistics reflect, there is a great need for healing and restoration. The victims and the perpetrators are in need of a way out of the bondage and the traumatic state they are experiencing.

CHAPTER SIX

The Journey of Facts, Victim's Rights, and Indicators: "Molestation and Rape"

Rape Classifications and Statistics

In the teaching manual "Counseling the Sexually Abused," from Bethany First Church of the Nazarene, Bethany, Oklahoma, Class Workshop (Training), "Prevention and Healing of Sexual Abuse," the following classifications of rape victims are defined as (depending on the victim's reaction to the rape):

(1) Rape Trauma Syndrome: The victim will react in acute anger.

(2) Compound Reaction: The victims who deal with more intense symptoms such as severe depression, suicidal behavior, or drug use.

(3) Silent Rape Reaction: The victims will be withdrawn or demonstrate repression.

(This writer suffered from the latter of the aforementioned—Silent Rape Reaction.)

As stated in "A Report to the Nation, National Victim Center," rape is called "the most underreported violent crime in America. Approximately one out of every six rapes has been reported to the police." In a study conducted by the Department of Justice and the Centers for Disease Control and prevention, researchers found that one in six women had experienced an attempted rape or completed rape. In the Rape in

America Study, 60 percent of the women who reported being raped were under eighteen years of age. Twenty-nine point three percent were less than eleven years old, 32.3 percent were between eleven and seventeen, and 22.2 percent were between twenty-five and twenty-nine. Six point one percent were older than twenty-nine, and 3.0 percent age was not available. From a report on Violence Against Women based on data from the National Crime Victimization Survey, Bureau of Justice Statistics, acquaintance rape is much more prevalent than stranger rape. In a study published by the Department of Justice, 82 percent of the victims were raped by someone they knew (acquaintance/friend, intimate, relative), and 18 percent were raped by a stranger.[1]

According to RAINN (Rape, Abuse, and Incest National Network), one in six women in America will be a victim of sexual assault. Seventeen point seven percent American women have been the victim of attempted or completed rape. Nine of every ten rape victims were female in 2003. Fourteen point eight percent of reported rapes are completed rape, and 2.8 percent are attempted rape. The majority of sexual assault victims are under thirty. Ages twelve to thirty-four are the highest risk years for rape and sexual assault. Those over seventy-five and older are 9 percent less likely than twelve to thirty-four-year-olds to be a victim of rape or sexual assault, and 83 percent less likely than twenty-five to forty-nine-year-olds. Women and girls experience sexual violence at high rates. Of American men, one in thirty-three or 3 percent has experienced an attempted or completed rape in their lifetime. One out of every ten rape victims is male. Sexual violence affects thousands of prisoners across the country. Sixty percent of all sexual violence against inmates is perpetrated by jail and prison staff while in prison or jail. More than 50 percent of the sex-

1 Copyright © 2004-06. Office of Health Education. University of Pennsylvania. Designed by Steve McCann.

ual contact between inmates and staff members—all of which is illegal—is non-consensual. Sexual violence in the military often goes unreported. In 2018 an estimated 20,500 sexual assaults occurred in the military. DOD estimates 62 percent of active-duty women and 0.7 percent of active-duty men experienced sexual assault in the year 2001. Native Americans are at the greatest risk of sexual violence. On average, American Indians ages twelve and older experience 5,900 sexual assaults per year. American Indians are twice as likely to experience rape/sexual assault compared to all races. Forty-one percent of sexual assaults against American Indians are committed by a stranger, 34 percent by an acquaintance, and 25 percent by an intimate or family member. All information is taken from RAINN Statistics of Victims of Sexual Violence.

The following information is taken from the teaching manual "Counseling the Sexually Abused," from Bethany First Church of the Nazarene, Bethany, Oklahoma, Class Workshop (Training), "Prevention and Healing of Sexual Abuse."

Responses to post-rape include *fear* of embarrassment, guilt, suspicion, and anger; *fear* of being alone, of crowds, of men, of anything reminding them of their assailant, of threats by their assailant; *fear* of spouse, family, friends, and others finding out; *fear* of venereal disease, of becoming pregnant; preoccupation with the assault, the disarray of normal sex life, crying, and being silent. Rape victims do need to talk about the offensive attacks because they cannot receive healing until they talk about it. Rape victims need to be aware of their rights after the assault takes place. These rights include but are not limited to the right to report the sexual offense to the police, the right to be examined by a female law enforcement officer, the right to report the crime without prosecuting, the right to withdraw testimony against the attacker, the right to reasonable witness protection, and the right to request copies of police reports.

My therapist, Delta Wilkerson, informed me of much information regarding abuse, rape, and violation of trust during my two years of counseling sessions. She gave me assignments to work on weekly for my next session, asking me to write down this information and reflect on these words to understand why I experienced many different emotions from my abuse and violations. Sexual abuse is when someone pressures, manipulates or forces another person into sexual activity. The two most common ways a person is pressured into sexual activity are bribes and threats. Many children and adults in our world today suffer from the physical and mental pain of sexual abuse. There are numerous ways sexual abuse can be defined, including verbal, visual, emotional, mental, and/or physical. The aforementioned sexual activities can be engaged in without consent, which may be emotionally or physically harmful and can exploit a person's sexual or emotional needs. I will focus on sexual abuse in which a person does not consent and is forced. In the article "Surviving Sexual Assault and Rape," based on a study published by the Department of Justice,

> Rape is actually defined as a forced, violent destructive/abusive treatment, sexual penetration against the victim's will and without consent. Rape is a crime of violence and is motivated by the desire to control or to have power over the victim. Rape is not about feelings of affection or love. Rape is the penetration of the female sex organ by a finger, a male sex organ, or by any object without consent. Consent is

based on choice and is possible only when there is equal power. Giving in because of fear is not consent. Going along with the crowd is not consent. If you can't say no comfortably, then yes has no meaning. Again, being unable to object to the act does not constitute consent and generally adheres to the same situations listed above for rape. Sexual battery is defined as unlawful, intentional touching without the consent of the victim with the intent of arousing or satisfying the sexual desires of the offender or another. As in the case of rape, sexual battery can occur in situations where the victim does not or could not object to the touching.

I believe rape is a betrayal of mankind. According to the United States Federal Bureau of Investigation (FBI), "a rape is reported about once every five minutes. Research reveals that any man is capable of rape. The average age of a rape victim is eighteen years old. There is no biological cause for a person to commit rape. The majority of abusers have been abused themselves."

Some children may suffer from the parent being absent from the home (father or mother) due to work, active social life, or neglect. The child may feel abandoned when the parent is not present in the child's life due to divorce, separation, or neglect, or lack of emotional security, nurturing, stimulation such as hugs, and activities such as playing, reading, conversing, and singing with their children. Children need love, security, acceptance, and time with their parents and families. This may result in the child having a strong need to control or develop the need to dominate.

The victim of rape and abuse must confess, repent, and forgive their perpetrator for true healing to take place. In chapter 7, the topic of forgiveness will be discussed. The Bible states in Exodus 34:7 that the sins of the father are visited upon their children to the third and fourth generations. We must not harbor unforgiveness, bitterness, or anger toward others. Rape is discussed in God's Word. Listed are a couple of passages that discuss rape; however, there are more than listed. Deuteronomy 22:25–27 and 2 Samuel 13:1–22. It is so important that abused and rape victims understand that God loves them and cares for them unconditionally. In previous chapters, I shared how I struggled with how God could allow these things to happen to me; however, He lovingly showed me how important I was to Him.

Mankind does not have the right to judge the rape victim. The church needs to adopt the victims unconditionally without judgment or gossip. They need to be loved, rescued, protected, encouraged, and shown mercy, grace, and compassion. They need to be comforted.

> Who forgives all your sins and heals all your diseases, who redeems your life from the pit and crowns you with love and compassion, who satisfies your desires with good things so that your youth is renewed like the eagle's. The Lord works righteousness and justice for all the oppressed. He made known his ways to Moses, his deeds to the people of Israel: The Lord is compassionate and gracious, slow to anger, abounding in love. He will not always accuse, nor will he harbor his anger forever; he does not treat us as our sins deserve or repay us according to our iniquities, For as high as the heavens are above the earth, so great is his love for those who fear him. God is their refuge and listener.
>
> Psalm 103:3–11 (KJV)

Hebrew 4:16 (KJV): "Let us then approach the throne of grace with confidence, so that we may receive mercy and find grace to help us in our time of need."

We must restore the victim's mind through the Word of God (Romans 12:2) and lead them to a point of forgiveness toward their perpetrator and themselves. We must forgive our trespassers seventy times seven. God teaches us this in Matthew 18:21–22 (KJV): "Then Peter came to Jesus and asked, 'Lord, how many times shall I forgive my brother when he sins against me? Up to seven times?' Jesus answered, 'I tell you, not seven times, but seventy times seven."

Stages of Adjustment

The following information was prepared by YWCA Intervention Services, Oklahoma City, Oklahoma, and adapted from "Raped" by Deborah Roberts.[2]

Each person going through a crisis of any kind progresses through stages of emotional adjustment. A victim may spend a great deal of time in one stage and only touch lightly on another or may pass through a number of the stages over and over again, each time experiencing them with a different intensity. Furthermore, anyone close to the victim may experience these stages as well.

SHOCK..."I'M NUMB."

Offering information to the victim during this stage is not helpful, as she will most likely remember very little, if anything, about what occurred during this time.

---

2 Deborah Roberts. "Raped." Zondervan Publishing House, 1981, 157–159.

DENIAL...............“THIS CAN'T HAVE HAPPENED.”

Not yet able to face the severity of the crisis, the victim spends time during this stage gathering strength. The period of denial serves as a cushion for the more difficult stages of adjustment which follow.

ANGER.........………........ “WHAT DID I DO/WHY ME?”

Much of the anger may be a result of the victim's feeling of loss of strength and loss of control over her own life. The anger may be directed toward the rapist, a doctor, the police, or anyone else, including herself.

BARGAINING...“LET'S GO ON AS IF IT DIDN'T HAPPEN.”

The victim sets up a bargain: She will not talk about the rape in exchange for not having to continue to experience the pain. In so doing, she continues to deny the emotional impact the rape has had upon her life.

DEPRESSION...“I FEEL SO DIRTY—SO WORTHLESS.”

If the victim is warned of this stage ahead of time, she may not be so thrown by it. She may experience drastic changes in sleeping or eating habits, indulging in compulsive rituals, or generalized fears completely taking over her life. Professional counseling may be advisable. Though a painful time for her, this stage shows she has begun to face the reality of the rape. As she allows the negative emotions to surface, she should be reminded that these feelings are normal and will not last forever.

ACCEPTANCE .... “LIFE CAN GO ON.”

(this is the first step to healing)

When enough of the anger and depression is released, the victim enters the state of acceptance. She may still spend time thinking and talking about the rape, but she understands and is in control of her own emotions and can now accept what has happened to her.

ASSIMILATION............ "IT'S PART OF MY LIFE."

By the time the victim reaches this stage, she has realized her own self-worth and strength. She no longer needs to spend time dealing with the rape, as the total rape experience now meshes with other experiences in her life.

Indicators of Child Sexual Abuse

None of the following behaviors in and of themselves indicates that a child is an incest/rape/abused victim, but two or more indicators should alert one to this possibility and the need to explore the situation with the child.

1. Excessive masturbation. Excessive masturbation is not only symptomatic of an extraordinary interest in the child's own sexuality but may also be a subconsciously motivated practice aimed at calling others' attention to the abusive situation. It is clearly a symbolic signal that there is something inappropriate in the child's psychosexual development. Additionally, a child may masturbate constantly to relieve the itch and discomfort of a venereal disease.

2. Overt sexual acting out toward adults. Adults who molest children often tell them that sex between adults and children is a permissible and accepted way of showing love. Incest victims, therefore, often make sexual advances toward adults they like because they have been taught that it is appropriate because they have come to associate nurturance with sexuality through their molestation experiences. They believe that they must provide sexual gratification to adults in order to receive love.

3. Simulation of sophisticated sexual activity with younger

children. Although boys and girls may not acknowledge that their molestation of younger children is done in an effort to communicate their own victimization to persons outside their family, it is our contention that their behavior is subconsciously motivated toward this end.

4. Fear of being alone with an adult, either male or female. Children who have been molested have often been told by the molester that they are irresistible, and they come to believe that all adults will be unable to control the impulse to molest them.

5. Violence against younger children. Incest/rape victims cannot safely express the anger and frustration they feel toward the molesting adult and will displace these feelings onto safer objects, such as younger children. They may also displace anger onto "safe" adults, such as teachers.

6. Self-mutilation. Child victims often develop feelings of self-hatred related to their powerlessness to defend themselves from incestuous assaults. This loss of self-respect may be expressed in a lot of different ways. (One is guilt.)

7. Bruises and hickeys or both in the face or neck area or around the groin, buttocks, and inner thighs. It is not unusual for incest/rape victims to have numerous bruises or hickeys on their bodies administered during molestation incidents. Often the bruises are the results of violence in response to the child's resisting the assault, and the hickeys may demonstrate varying degrees of redness, indicating that they were not all administered at the same time.

8. Fear of bathrooms and showers. (Number one place for abuse.) Sexually abused victims are frightened of bathrooms and showers because these are the places where they are most often molested. Under the pretense of helping the child with his or her bath, parents and relatives often use such opportunities to molest the child.

9. Knowledge of sexual matters and details of adult sexual activity inappropriate to age or developmental level. Children experience being molested as violence even when they are not physically injured. They, therefore, express a great deal of anger and pain in describing it, whether in words, art, or play. Molested children report having communicated their incest problem to teachers and others in their schoolwork, honestly expecting that adult professionals would interpret their messages requesting help.

10. Extreme fear or repulsion when touched by an adult of either sex. Sexually abused victims do not associate a nurturing touch with pleasure or safety. Such touching has been foreplay for them, or what has led up to molestation situations. Being touched affectionately by an adult is, therefore, unlikely to be pleasurable; rather, it is threatening and terrifying.

11. Refusal to undress for physical education class at school. Sexually abused victims believe people can tell just by looking at their bodies that they have been molested, so they are unwilling to be seen naked by others. Also, they have often been told by the molester that their bodies are irresistible and that molester cannot keep from molesting them. The children, therefore, fear that if they are seen nude, other people may lose control and molest them.

NOTE: I have included more information and lists of behavioral indicators in an addendum at the end of this book.

CHAPTER SEVEN

The Journey of Forgiveness: "When I Prayed Through and Trusted and Obeyed"

As I prayed for my healing, God prompted me to make a list of all who had abused me in some way. I ended up with twenty-six names of those who had abused me either physically, mentally, verbally, emotionally, financially, or sexually. I never realized how many had somehow abused me. I even remembered a coach in junior high school who constantly made inappropriate remarks about my physique. It is amazing how many hurtful and devastating events the Holy Spirit revealed to me. God showed me I had to forgive all who had hurt me. My first response was, "I was the victim, so why did I have to forgive them?" The Holy Spirit strongly convinced me about the forgiveness issue.

I was praying one morning, and God impressed me to drive to the town where the butcher lived who molested me at the age of twelve. I did not want to see him. The memory of what he had done brought up angry feelings. I told God I shouldn't have to go see him, but I felt led to do this. I hesitantly got in my car and headed in that direction. I did not understand why I had to forgive him, but God reminded me of how many times He had forgiven me. I had no idea what I was going to say or how I was going to act.

I pulled into the parking lot of the grocery store where he worked. The store was all locked up, and the building was empty. I felt so much relief. I thought I was off the hook on this one. I decided to drive through the town to see how it had changed. As I was driving, I saw a grocery store with the name that used to be on the old building I had driven to previously. My stomach tightened with so many knots, and fear and anger overcame me.

I reluctantly pulled into the parking lot, wondering if he was inside. The Holy Spirit let me know he was there. I sat there for a little while and asked God why I had to do this. God showed me this had nothing to do with how "I" felt; this was a choice I had to make.

Then, God reminded me of the story about the lame man by the pool of Bethesda (Bethesda means "house of mercy"). He reminded me of the passage that said, "Do you really want to be healed?" (John 5:1–15, KJV). I told God yes, I wanted to be healed. He prompted me, "Then, you have to forgive." God always expects action on our part.

As I reflected on this story, the details came to mind. There was a great multitude of sick people, blind, lame, paralyzed, waiting for the moving of the water. The angel went down at a certain time into the pool and stirred the water, then whoever stepped in first, after the stirring of the water, was made well of whatever disease they had. Jesus walked onto the scene and healed only one man (John 5:5–6). This is the verse Jesus asked this man who had an infirmity for thirty-eight years, "Do you want to be healed?" Do you think that is an unusual question to ask a man who has been ill for thirty-eight years? In verse seven, the sick man answered Him, "Sir, I have no man to put me into the pool when the water is stirred; but while I am coming, another steps down into the water before me." The man answers Jesus with an excuse. He says, "Yes, I want to be healed, but I can't; I've tried, and I've done everything I know to do. I want to get into the water, and I want to be healed, but

I lack the ability. I have no one to help me."

Have you given up on your situation? Have you embraced your woundedness, hurt, pain, etc.? Many people are right where this man was, with a sense of hopelessness about making any change in their lives. What kind of help does Jesus offer wounded people? He told the lame man to "Rise, take up your bed and walk!" Jesus just says, "Get up!" So, the lame man could obey His command or just stay lame. Jesus' next command was, "Walk!" If the lame man wanted to be healed, he had to get up and walk away from the pool. He had to walk by faith in another direction and walk away from his lameness. The man obeyed; he took up his bed and walked. It took action on his part. He was healed. Jesus has all the answers for our lives. It doesn't matter what situation it is, He has healing for all of us, and we have to accept or reject His blessings. We are not to rely on our feelings or understanding. We have to have complete trust in Him. "Prepare your mind for action" (1 Peter 1:13a, KJV). If we are going to be ready for Christ's return, then we better be mentally alert, disciplined, have self-control, and be focused. All that Christ requires of us is to take action, responsibility, and accountability.

I had to do this God's way if I wanted to be healed; I could no longer do things my way. I had to obey God's command to forgive. Was this hard for me to do? Yes, because of my lack of understanding of how forgiving this man would give me freedom. I had to make a choice at that moment if I wanted to be healed. I had to trust God's way because my way was not helping me at all. All I felt was anger toward this man. I begrudgingly opened the car door, got out, and walked into the store. The next thought that entered my mind was, "Maybe he doesn't work here anymore." I proceeded to the back of the store, and there he was. My heart fell to the floor, and I couldn't breathe for a few seconds. He was waiting on customers, and so I patiently waited until all were gone. There I was, standing with no one else for him to wait on, and he said, "May I help you?" I then asked him if he remembered me. And he said, "No, do I know you?" Needless to say, anger whaled up inside of me like a volcano, ready to erupt. I thought, *That's great; he doesn't even remember me.* I took a deep breath and said, "I'm the little girl you molested in my front yard many years ago; my name is Marylin." He turned all shades of red and then white. I took a deep breath once again and said, "I came to say two things to you; first, I want to tell you I forgive you for what you did to me; secondly, I want to tell you Jesus loves you and forgives you too." At that moment, I felt total peace. I told him, "I will pray for you to know Jesus and have peace in your life and for you to forgive yourself but to remember that Jesus loves you and wants a relationship with you." I then turned and walked out of the store with the biggest smile on my face. I felt total freedom and was instantly released from all anger, hurt, shame, and fear. I peeled off the pain and placed it back in the original source. I had been set free, but my part wasn't complete. I continue to pray for him when I think about this moment. I pray he has accepted Christ and asked Jesus for forgiveness and for God to extend mercy to him. I don't know what he went through in his life or what he endured as a child. I have to remember hurting people hurt others. I ask Jesus when he comes to my mind, and I'm lifting him up in prayer for Jesus to extend love, mercy, grace, forgiveness, and healing to him.

I now realized why I had to forgive him. It wasn't for him; it was for me! Just like the man at the Pool of Bethesda, he had to get up and exert action to be healed. When we obey God's Word, God extends His grace and mercy to us. My mother used to tell me to remember that grace is getting what we do not deserve, salvation, forgiveness, healing, and eternal life. Mercy is not getting what we do deserve, judgment or punishment. Jesus is asking us to look to Him and Him alone for our healing. This requires forgiveness toward our perpetrator.

I drove by the house where we lived when this event happened, and I felt total peace. I sang all the way home and thought of all my perpetrators and abusers and asked God do I have to go to everyone who has offended me? He graciously said, "No, Marylin, all that is required is to forgive them," and at that moment, I chose to forgive all those who trespassed against me, and I said a prayer for each perpetrator. I wept tears of joy as the chains of bondage broke and fell, and I experienced true joy and peace. Wow! God is so good to us, and if we listen to His voice, we will be healed beyond measure.

Forgiveness is the only strategic modality to glorious freedom. I encourage everyone to make a list today of all who have hurt you and choose to forgive. This does not mean that you condone what has been done to you; it is a means to set you free from the torment, trauma, chaos, despair, damaged emotions, hurt, shame, depression, false guilt, low self-esteem, and unforgiveness. By making the choice to forgive, you destroy all that the enemy has brought against you. God's way is the only way to a victorious life!

The following is a handout that I was given when attending Vinelife Ministries Biblical Counseling Classes in Oklahoma City around the year 1999 to 2000. The handout was given to us by Norma Johnson of Beyond Restoration Ministries, Intl., Oklahoma City, Oklahoma.

The Key Is Forgiveness

Unforgiveness is the lock and key that keeps us in bondage. The key that unlocks freedom is forgiveness. We will examine some reasons we have unforgiveness and how we can use the key of forgiveness to open the door to freedom.

A. CAUSES OF UNFORGIVENESS:

1. The parent/person who never gave praise but was quick to criticize.

2. The unfair boss who handed out the pink slip.

3. The spouse who was unfaithful.

4. The bully who was verbally, physically, or emotionally abusive.

5. The spouse who was verbally, physically, sexually, or emotionally abusive.

6. The parent who was verbally, physically, sexually, or emotionally abusive.

7. The school teacher, Sunday school teacher, who was verbally, physically, sexually, or emotionally abusive or critical and unfair.

8. Any other person who was verbally, physically, sexually, or emotionally abusive.

9. The parent who was never there to guide you and protect you.

10. The parent or spouse who abandoned you physically or emotionally.

These are people who inflicted hurts on us that may take years to overcome. We may hold a grudge or never overcome what was done to us. We say the worst things to them—or brood over what we wish we'd said. We want revenge. We ask, why should I forgive them? They hurt me. I did nothing wrong! I should not have to forgive those who inflicted pain and heartache on me. I am the victim, so why do I have to forgive? Sound familiar?

B. HOW DO WE KNOW WE HAVE UNFORGIVENESS?

SIGNS OF UNFORGIVENESS
(a few examples—there are many more)

*Abusive Actions

*Anger

*Avoid Close Relationships

*Bitterness

*Blame Others
(When things happen to you)

*Bully Others

*Controlling

*Critical of Others

*Demanding

*Depression

*Disrespectful

*Fear

*Hatred of Others

*Hurt

*Jealousy

*Judgmental

*Low Self-Esteem

*Negative Personality

*Oppression

*Rejection (reject others)

*Resentment

*Sabotage Relationships

*Self Hatred

*Selfish (it's all about me)

*Sinful Nature
(Unconfessed Sin)

*Suicidal Thoughts

*Unkind Comments

*Victim Mentality, Attitude

*Vindictive

*Withdrawal

C. HOW DOES UNFORGIVENESS WORK?

When we hold a person in bondage (or hostage) by unforgiveness, we withhold:

1. Love

2. Acceptance

3. Respect

The message we send them is that until I feel you have repaid me for the wrong done to me, you will not have my acceptance, love, or respect. When we refuse to forgive, we refuse to cancel the debt, and that puts us in bondage.

D. WHY DO WE NOT FORGIVE?

1. Fear we will be hurt again.

2. Belief that we will be condoning the action or person that caused the hurt.

3. Belief that we have a right not to forgive.

4. Belief that we want the other person to suffer the same or worse hurt.

5. Belief that others will think we are fools if we forgive.

6. Prideful. I am above forgiveness.

E. WAYS PEOPLE TRY TO FORGIVE BUT ARE UNABLE:

1. "I just won't think about it, or I'll try to understand." The problem is that something new always reminds us of the past.

2. "I just won't let it hurt me as much." Some new event reopens the wound, and it hurts.

"I did forgive the person/action, but they keep doing the same thing over and over." Therefore, I do not know how to keep forgiving the same problem.

F. WHY DO WE NEED TO FORGIVE?

1. Matthew 6:14–15 (NIV): "For if you forgive men when they sin against you, your heavenly Father will also forgive you. But if you do not forgive men their sins, your Father will not forgive your sins."

2. Matthew 18:21–35 (NIV): Then Peter came to Jesus and asked, Lord, how many times shall I forgive my brother when he sins against me: Up to seven times? Jesus answered, I tell you, not seven times, but seventy times seven. Therefore, the kingdom of heaven is like a king who wanted to settle accounts with his servants. As he began the settlement, a man who owed him ten thousand talents was brought to him. Since he was not able to pay, the master ordered that he and his wife and his children and all that he had be sold to repay the debt. The servant fell on his knees before him. Be patient with me, he begged, and I will pay back everything. The servant's master took pity on him, canceled the debt and let him go. But when that servant went out, he found one of his fellow servants who owed him a hundred denarii. He grabbed him and began to choke him. Pay back what you owe me! He demanded. His fellow servant fell to his knees and begged him, Be patient with me, and I will pay you back. But he refused. Instead, he went off and had the man thrown into prison until he could pay the debt. When the other servants saw what had happened, they were greatly distressed and went and told their master everything that had happened. Then the master called the servant in. You wicked servant, he said, I canceled all that debt

of yours because you begged me to. Shouldn't you have had mercy on your fellow servant just as I had on you? In anger his master turned him over to the jailers to be tortured, until he should pay back all he owed. This is how my heavenly Father will treat each of you unless you forgive your brother from your heart.

HOW DO WE FORGIVE?

G. HOW TO FORGIVE WHEN OFFENDED:

1. Recognize and receive God's personal love and forgiveness for you (1 John 4:6–11, 16–19).

2. Recognize that Christ is Lord; He is in control (Ephesians 1:19–23).

3. Have a positive attitude toward the offense. What is important is not who or what offended us but that we respond correctly to the situation (Philippians 2:14–18; 4:4).

4. Realize that God is working through the actions of your offender. The offender is simply an instrument in God's hand to accomplish His ultimate will in your life (Genesis 50:20; Philippians 2:13).

5. Thank God for each offense. Discern what benefits and character qualities God wants to develop in your life through the offense (1 Thessalonians 5:18; Romans 8:28–29; Galatians 5:22–23).

6. Recognize that bitterness is assuming a right we don't have (Romans 12:17–21).

7. By faith (not by feelings), choose to forgive the offender. Verbalize this choice. For exam-

ple, "Lord, in obedience to Your Word, I choose by faith to forgive _____for _____. I trust You to change my feelings and wrong thoughts. Amen." Repeat this as necessary, as many times as it takes to let the wrong done to you go. Every time you have a thought regarding the wrong done to you, repeat this prayer.

8. Cooperate with God in healing the offender's life by returning good for evil. (1 Thessalonians 5:15; Romans 12:21)

9. Seek Godly counseling if you are not able to get victory from these steps.

H. HOW DO WE CONTINUE TO LIVE IN FORGIVENESS AFTER WE HAVE SUCCESSFULLY DEALT WITH PAST PROBLEMS?

1. How can we continue to forgive when we are in a hurting relationship?

A. The husband or wife that is verbally or emotionally abusive?

B. A parent that can't be pleased?

C. A boss that continually puts you down?

Understanding the pressures and problems these persons are under can help us to continually forgive while we pray for them to change. This is very hard and a test of our faith, but we know what Jesus' answer was in Matthew 18:21–22: "'Then Peter came to Jesus and asked, "Lord, how many times shall I forgive my brother when he sins against me? Up to seven times?' Jesus answered, 'I tell you, not seven times, but seventy times seven.'"

[End of handout]

We need to understand that to forgive does not mean to give in. It means to let go. Once you forgive, you are no longer emotionally entwined with the person who hurt you. You are set free from the bondage of pain, hurt, torment, trauma, etc., that was imposed on you. Forgiveness sets you free of someone else's nightmare, hurt, pain, etc., and allows you to live in a state of grace. If forgiveness feels so good, why do so many people go around in bitterness? People feel like they will lose their sense of power if they let go of the hurt. We feel more in charge when we have anger. Some think forgiving means saying they are wrong and the other person was right, but forgiving is not letting someone off the hook, it is about taking the hurt, pain, anger, bitterness, and all unforgiveness out of your own heart. It can free you from the bitterness of the hurt you feel. Many times the person who hurt you may not even be aware of what they have done, and you are being tormented by anger and hurt. It is up to you to forgive and let go of the debt they owe you. Remember, you are the one who is hurting. It can cause you to be physically sick. Depression is always present when you don't forgive. Also, remember that hurting people hurt people. Forgiving does not mean you condone what has been done to you. It only means that you choose not to hang on to the pain they put on you. Jesus said to those who tortured, beat, and rejected him, cursed him, spit on him, and mocked him, "Father forgive them for they know not what they do" (Luke 23:34, KJV). Jesus suffered more than anyone, and He chose to forgive. He died for you and me as well as for the one who does the injustice to others. He died so all could be forgiven and set free from the bondage of abuse, whether emotional, physical, verbal, or sexual. We are free by the precious blood of the Lamb! Forgiveness is a choice. I choose this day to forgive all who have come against me. Thank You, Jesus, for Your love and forgiveness for all my trespasses.

(This section below was on the handout.)

LIST WHAT YOU REAP/GAIN BY NOT FORGIVING:

_____

_____

_____

_____

LIST WHAT YOU REAP/GAIN IF YOU DO FORGIVE:

_____

_____

_____

_____

(How does it hurt YOU by not forgiving?)

_____

_____

_____

_____

(What do YOU lose?)

_____

_____

_____

_____

I NEED TO FORGIVE.......... FOR THE OFFENCE
THAT HURT ME.

NAME: OFFENCE:

_____   _____

_____   _____

_____   _____

_____   _____

_____   _____

_____   _____

_____   _____

_____   _____

_____   _____

_____   _____

_____   _____

* End of the handout.

Dear Lord:

I choose to forgive _____

for _____

_____

I will cancel their debts/trespasses just as Christ canceled my debts/trespasses. I release them to You, Lord, and You are their Judge and mine. I will trust You, Lord, to heal my hurts and offenses. Thank You, Jesus, for releasing me from this bondage and setting me free. I surrender my life to You and choose love, peace, forgiveness, and joy. Amen.

Date: _____

Now, you can let the pain and bondage go. You are free of the pain they instilled upon you. You now have a responsibility to let them go from your life.

You may even have to separate yourself from them and lean 100 percent on Jesus Christ. I choose Christ, not pain and hurt and bondage. Thank You, Jesus, for giving me the strength to overcome through forgiveness. Now, Jesus is Lord of my life.

CHAPTER EIGHT

The Journey from False Guilt to Shame to Healing: "On a Personal Note"

G uilt is the result of having violated a specific rule or statute when we cross a moral, ethical, or legal boundary. According to the Bible, we are all guilty before God (Romans 3:10, 23). What is the difference between guilt, false guilt, and shame? Guilt is a feeling one gets when doing something wrong. Making bad choices is an example of guilt. Simply one word can describe guilt: wrongness. Guilt is heaviness, an unbearable burden that depresses our spirit. Guilt makes us feel tired and weary, drawing our energy and strength. Guilt causes us to be weak therefore making it difficult to resist sin and the thoughts that Satan puts upon us. The devil wants us to feel "wrong" about ourselves, and he wants to prevent us from enjoying our relationship with God and His Son, Jesus Christ. We should not let Satan rob our faith. Stay strong by reading God's Word and trusting Jesus to give us strength. We were created by God to feel right and good regarding our life, both inward and outward. Due to the fall of man, we cannot do everything right. When we accept Jesus as Lord of our life, He gives us the gift of righteousness. God sent His Son, Jesus, to redeem us. "Therefore there is now no condemnation for those who are in Christ Jesus" (Romans 8:1, KJV). Let go of the guilt.

In my situation, guilt was a false feeling of rejection and condemnation. True guilt is when we are separated from God, and we are deserving of condemnation for sin. Our condemnation for sin can only be removed through Jesus Christ. When we have false guilt, we must repeat Romans 8:1 until we believe it in our hearts and minds, "Therefore there is now no condemnation (false guilt) for those who are in Christ Jesus."

Shame is a negative emotion that combines feelings of dishonor, unworthiness, and embarrassment. Shame can be healthy at times. If I hurt someone or break something that belongs to another, then I feel ashamed of my mistake or wrongdoing. I may feel that I was negligent, and I am sorry for what I did. There is another type of shame that can affect the quality of our life. This can occur when an individual is being abused, bullied, or mistreated. In this instance, we may internalize the feelings we are subjected to. We take on these feelings of shame that have been put upon us, thus causing us to be frustrated or confused. If we take the time to think about these words, guilt, false guilt, and shame, in the right perspective, we may discover that the root of our problem is shame and not guilt.

Through shame, we don't like who we are. We may try to be something or someone we can never be. When Jesus showed me that I was putting a lower standard on my life through shame, I was saying that what He did for me was not enough. He died so I could be free from all bondages of shame. The Holy Spirit showed me several scriptures that helped me to be delivered from the spirit of shame. Psalm 25:20–21 (Zondervan Life Application Bible), "Guard my life and rescue me, let me not be put to shame, for I take refuge in you. May integrity and uprightness protect me, because my hope is in you." Isaiah 54:4 (Zondervan Life Application Bible), "Do not be afraid; you will not suffer shame. Do not fear disgrace; you will not be humiliated, You will forget the shame of your youth and remember no more the reproach of your widowhood." Isaiah 61:7 (Zondervan Life Application Bible), "Instead of their shame my people will receive a double portion, and instead of disgrace they will rejoice in their inheritance; so they will inherit a double portion in their land, and everlasting joy will be theirs." God can deliver us from shame and keep our thoughts pure in Him. When shame comes upon us, we need to pray and ask God to give us strength and build up our faith. And trust in His Word. In Nehemiah 8:10b (Zondervan Life Application Bible), God tells us, "The joy of the Lord is your strength." To receive our healing, we must trust God and believe the scriptures He has given us to overcome false guilt and shame. The guilt that the enemy puts on us is not real. We must fill our hearts and minds with the Word of God to be victorious and "Now choose life so that you and your children may live" (Deuteronomy 30:19, Zondervan Life Application Bible).

When traumatic events interrupt our lives, we suffer in a world that seems dark and tragic. Sometimes we ask ourselves, "How could God allow this to happen to me?" Somehow, through our tragedies, we lose hope. "How can I be the same after this hurt?" Then, we lose love. "How can I give and receive when so much has been lost?" Loss of faith, hope, and love causes us to suffer and lose even more friendships, the ability to *not* get ahead, and causes us to have frustration, not get along with others, low self-esteem, shame, and guilt. Even if we pray and strive toward God, the battles of life seem to drain our faith, hope, and love.

What is faith? Faith is believing and putting doubts away. What is hope? Hope is merely turning away from despair and being positive. What is love? Love is plainly stated in 1 Corinthians 13, which involves being kind and not letting disappointment make us bitter. Once we come to the place of dying to self as we walk across the dry desert where things don't make sense (lack of understanding of the heartaches), we can go through the valley and conquer. When we go through the dry desert, it is lonely and barren, making us feel rejected and doleful. It is the place where the lives of the banished by God roam, awaiting eternal damnation. The life of banishment is for unbelief and rebellion. We must not allow ourselves to stay in the desert. We must persevere and endure allowing ourselves to push forward through the valley and conquer.

Doubt, tragedies, and disappointments are a part of our daily life, and these are the tools God uses to help us grow in faith, hope, and love. These are also the tools Satan uses to tear us down. However, it is our choice what tools we pick up and how we use them. We can pick up God's tools and use them to build hope, love, and faith and to do God's will in our lives. If we choose Satan's tools and hold on to them, we will not be the person God wants us to be, and Satan will use these tools to kill, steal and destroy our lives. If we run or hide from these fears, we are cheating ourselves of the destiny God has for us.

The roses are among the thorns (a thorn in the biblical sense is a symbol of trouble, the cares of this world, and spiritual affliction), and the beautiful flowers are among the weeds, but if we overlook and overcome the weeds and thorns, then the beauty and face of God shine through. With God, our disappointments, despairs, betrayals, and weaknesses, somehow force us to move upward to a greater path or destination. God has given us the capacity to find a better road to our destiny in spite of all the tragedies that come our way. There have been many thorns and weeds in my life. The most devastating of all have been the molestations, rapes, and spousal abuse that had shattered my life beyond control. Others' decisions and choices changed the course of my life. These traumatic events altered my sound mind and replaced that with painful realities, hurt, fear, and confusion.

Satan is the father of lies (John 8:44) and had me believing that I would have to suffer all my life, although at a young age,

I chose to repress my feelings and shut out all the bad. I forced myself to smile, and I hid my pain well for years. I would always pick myself up and go forward in my high school years through Christ, praise and worship music, piano, church, and sports such as softball, basketball, volleyball, and track. Actually, I would participate in any activity to stay busy. I was successful at whatever I "threw" myself into, thus denying the pain, hurt, and confusion.

Unfortunately, we live in a culture that places a high value on individual accomplishment. Most of us have been encouraged by the idea of high achievement. Being competitive in school, sports, and business is viewed as important in our society. Our belief system has been corrupted with the idea that if we work hard enough, we will be winners and, therefore, good people. If we don't measure up, then we believe we are failures. We continue to allow our worth and self-esteem to be determined by what we do and what others think of us and not by who we are in Christ. The repression of events in my life and evil in this world did harm to my heart and, at times, clouded my love for God and others. I lived my life in my own mind, will, and emotions which were all damaged. Even though I was God's child, I had not taken hold of the thought that I was a new creation in Jesus, and I did not realize the depth of the love and power available to me in Christ. I had not fully comprehended the truths of Scripture. Jesus had paid the price for my sins as well as those of my perpetrators. Isaiah 53:3–5 states:

> He was despised and rejected by men, a man of sorrows, and familiar with suffering. Like one from whom men hid their faces he was despised, and we esteemed him not. Surely he took up our infirmities and carried our sorrows, yet we considered him stricken by God, smitten by him, and afflicted. But He was pierced for our transgressions, he was crushed for our iniquities, the punish-

ment that brought us peace was upon him, and by his wounds, we are healed.

Isaiah 53:3–5 (Zondervan Life Application Bible)

Jesus paid the price for my deliverance and forgiveness, but I did not have a clue how to receive His gracious gift of mercy, love, and forgiveness. As I remembered all that I had repressed, it never occurred to me that I was suffering from all these acts of abuse and rejection. I thought because I had repressed everything, all those events were in my past. These actions were no longer happening to me in the present, but it was still embedded in my inner being and in my emotions. As I recalled these circumstances, I felt the effects of them, thus needing the power of the Holy Spirit to endure and embrace all the pain and suffering. When we are experiencing pain, we should not fight it; we should allow it to accomplish its purpose. I had learned how to camouflage the ugly, painful side. This undoubtedly became a pattern in my life for years. Deep inside, I followed the path of sorrow and suffering, and on the outside, I followed the path of joy, peace, and success. However, God, in His own way, did encourage me and help me on this difficult journey. Without God, I could have become a drug addict, an alcoholic, or acted out in many other ways. I threw myself into anything that would keep my mind busy and not allow me to think about these things. So, my vice of choice was to stay busy.

God's perfect plan for His Son included suffering and pain. The difference in Christ was He was without sin, and He never lost sight of faith, hope, and love. I am thankful I kept my faith, hope, and love, although it did waiver at times. The body of Christ (the church) needs to provide a means for hurting people to identify emotions and talk about them without being judged or condemned. The church needs to be held accountable to surround all victims and perpetrators with love, acceptance, and compassion and encourage an intimate relationship by communicating our feelings to one another. This is the body of Christ's responsibility to provide security and acceptance to those who are suffering. No one in the body of Christ should ever feel rejected.

I know what my mother taught me from God's precious Word is "truth" because the steps that God took me through studying and meditating on His powerful Words in Scripture showed me the way. "Jesus saith unto him, 'I am the way the truth and the life'" (John 14:6, KJV). I have come to realize that God's timing is more productive than my timing. He placed me where he did for a reason.

The healing process came when "Marylin, the adult," was strong enough to listen to "Marylin, the child." In therapy, one of my assignments was "Marylin, the adult, had to write a letter to Marylin, the child," and tell her that she was now strong enough to know everything that happened to her as a child. When she came to the place where "God was the strongest part of her life," then, and only then, could she begin to deal with the traumas of her childhood."

I attended Vine Life Ministries for four semesters and realized this was to confirm what God had already shown me. The study of the manuals and the teachings removed the confusion in my life and opened the "understanding" of the healing process, thus deepening the power of the Holy Spirit in my life and giving me confidence and the belief in God and myself that I can help point others toward Christ that are in need of restoration and healing. I praise and thank God for this opportunity because my faith, hope, and love were strengthened. "And so abideth faith, hope, and charity" (1 Corinthians 13:13, KJV). Scope Ministries helped me to grow deeper in the Word and understand the transformation process, thus giving me strength and power in the Holy Spirit and the tools to teach others how to be totally transformed by the renewing of the mind through the Scriptures. Jim Craddock of Scope Ministries and The Billy Graham Evangelistic Association gave me the opportunity to do Crisis Counseling in New York City, New York, after the bombing of the Twin Towers (9/11). God's training has blessed my life through other's traumatic experiences, thus deepening my love for Christ even more. All trauma, terror, abuse, and attacks of evil can be turned around for good through Jesus Christ our Lord. God is a sovereign God, and we need to take heed of His supreme direction. Jesus is most definitely the only way to have total healing, joy, and peace. Through my healing process, Christ has prepared me for the mercy seat. He provided freedom from my past by enabling me to comprehend through the study of His Word. He brought me through the steps of healing and forgiveness once again, but in a "deeper, more organized, thorough, and understanding way."

I have wept before Him many times as I have studied, read His precious Words, and deepened my relationship with Him, thus profoundly increasing my appreciation of His love for me. I am finally able to relinquish my desire to be judge and jury over my life. I have learned to understand and accept God's complete forgiveness of my perpetrators and myself. The battle of my past has ended in victory as I have received deliverance and healing through God's Word. The strongholds have been broken, and God's presence has taken precedence over their existence.

I once suffered as a domestic violence/rape/abused victim, and I have been set free. I know without a doubt that God is the answer for rape/abused victims. I also know that God and His Son, Jesus, are the Deliverer and Healer of all sickness, traumas, tragedies, and pain. "For God hath not given us a spirit of fear; but of power, and of love and of a sound mind" (2 Timothy 1:7, KJV).

I thank my heavenly Father and His Son, Jesus Christ, for my victory! No truer words have been stated: "I am the Vine and ye are the branches, He that abideth in me, and I in Him, the same bringeth forth much fruit; for without Me ye can do nothing" (John 15:5, KJV). Also, "Being confident in this very thing, that He who began a good work in you (me) will perform it until the day of Jesus Christ" (Philippians 1:6, KJV). "For everything that was written in the past was written to teach us, so that through endurance and the encouragement of the Scriptures we might have hope" (Romans 15:4). I am blessed to have a mom who diligently taught me the Word of God as I was growing up.

CHAPTER NINE

The Foundation Journey:
"The Early Years and Ministry"

Ask yourself these questions in regards to your life.

Where and when were you born?

_____

_____

Describe the circumstances surrounding your birth.

_____

_____

Did you have any medical complications as a child?

_____

_____

_____

_____

Do you believe that you were an accident or a surprise to God?

_____

_____

_____

_____

Why do you believe this?

_____

_____

_____

_____

Marylin, at the age of three, a happy child before all the abuse began
in her life at age six.

(Jeremiah 29:11 [NIV]: "'For I know the plans I have for
you,' declares the LORD, 'plans to prosper you, and not to harm
you, plans to give you hope and a future.'")

I was the bouncing baby girl of a proud mother and father who, at the time of my birth, did not know Christ. My mother remembered her grandmother talking to her about Jesus and wanted me to have what she (my mom) never had. This piqued her curiosity, and she began to seek information regarding God and Jesus Christ. She came to know Christ at church one Sunday morning when the preacher was sharing about Noah and the Ark. He stated that when God shut the door to the ark, no one else could get inside. She did not want to be one that was left outside. She went forward, giving her heart to Christ, and was baptized, thus receiving the gift of eternal life.

This was the beginning of her spiritual foundation as well as mine. Regarding my father, my mom and I had been going to church since I was three years old, and I asked my mother (around the age of four), "Why did Daddy not come with us?" She said that was his choice and all we could do was pray for him. We began to pray every day for his salvation. God answered our prayers. He came to a revival meeting and accepted Christ, and was baptized. Due to my mother's determination to seek answers for her own life, our family was saved and given the gift of eternal life through Jesus Christ, our precious Lord. I know my mom and dad's reward will be in heaven with Jesus, and this gives me great peace and comfort.

Answer these questions about you and your family.

Were you planned?

_____

_____

_____

_____

Describe your mother.

_____

_____

_____

_____

_____

Describe your father.

_____

_____

_____

_____

_____

What were the spiritual beliefs in your family?

_____

_____

_____

_____

_____

Those who are loved and affirmed by their parents tend to have a healthy self-concept and find it easy to believe that God is loving and powerful. After my mother became a Christian, she and I became actively involved in church. She began to pray over me and read the Bible to me daily. At the age of six, in a church service, I gave my heart to Christ and was baptized. This was the greatest, most precious experience in my life. A missionary family was visiting our church, and after their testimony and sharing about the work God had called them to do, I knew deep in my heart this was what I wanted to be. I wanted to tell others about Jesus and help those in need.

Answer questions about your spiritual experiences as a child.

Did you have anyone praying for you or teaching you God's Word as a child?

_____

_____

_____

_____

Have you given your heart to Christ? If so, where, when, and what were the circumstances?

_____

_____

_____

_____

Have you been baptized?

_____

_____

If yes, when and where?

_____

_____

Mark 16:16: "He that believeth and is baptized shall be saved; but he that believeth not shall be damned." Romans 10:9 (KJV): "That if thou shalt confess with thy mouth the Lord Jesus, and shalt believe in thine heart that God hath raised Him from the dead, thou shalt be saved."

After giving my heart to Christ and being baptized, Christ birthed a deeper passion and compassion for others in me. Although, I always had the desire to help those less fortunate than myself. I had a friend at church diagnosed with polio. After church, she couldn't go outside to play with the other children, so I would always choose to stay inside and play with her. We would take turns going up and down the aisles as fast as we could on her crutches. I could also remember when she got a drink at the water fountain, pieces of her teeth would come out as she was drinking the water. I would always say to my mother and father, "I wish I could have crutches so that Judy wouldn't be alone and we could do the same things together."

Reflect on the following questions regarding others less fortunate than you.

How do you respond to those less fortunate?

Do you have compassion for them, make fun of them, or say hurtful things to them/about them?

How do you relate to those less fortunate than yourself?

_____

_____

_____

_____

Do you show them love and encouragement and offer words of kindness to them, or do you simply not care or have time for them?

_____

_____

_____

_____

Not only did I have compassion for the less fortunate, but God gave me a great desire to share about Christ so others could know him. I asked my parents if I could go to "skid row" to tell people about Jesus. My mother said that it was not a place for six-year-old girls. I persisted, and eventually, my father weakened and took me if I would agree to do exactly as I was told. We arrived downtown, and I wanted to go into the bar. Reluctantly, my dad took me inside. He picked me up and placed me on a barstool, and I spun it around a few times and then stood up on the stool and began to tell others about Jesus. I told them of His love for them and how He died on the cross so all could have eternal life.

There was an older man sitting at the bar drinking, and I began to talk to him. The questions I asked him did not come from a six-year-old child. They came from the Holy Spirit. I asked him why he was there drinking. He replied, "I don't know. Nothin' better to do." I asked him where his wife was and if he had any children, parents, brothers, or sisters. His reply was, "They are all dead. I have no one. My parents died, my brother was killed in the war, and my wife and children were killed in a car accident. I have no family left. No one cares or loves me." I told him how much Jesus loved him, enough to die for him, and, most importantly, Jesus loved him just as he was. I also asked him when was the last time he had eaten, and he said, "Three weeks ago." I asked Dad if we could take him to get something to eat. My dad said yes; there was a mission a couple of blocks away. We went there, and the gentleman ate, talked to the pastor who preached that evening after the service, and gave his heart to the Lord. They were baptizing a couple of others that evening. That night the man gave his heart to the Lord and was baptized. The next week I told my mother I wanted to go see how the old man was doing and talk to him again. My mom said he probably would not be there as that was not where he lived. I was persistent again, so my dad took me to the mission. The gentleman at the mission told my father that shortly after midnight (the very night we took him there), the older gentleman died. My dad said that Jesus was very happy that I cared about him. My mother told me I had a star on my crown. I loved helping others and caring about people. I would ask my dad to take me to hand out tracks and put them in restrooms and on cars. God had a special ministry in mind for me. I had already begun to damage Satan's plan for people to be a part of the kingdom of darkness by spreading the gospel of light. I believe that is when Satan and his helpers decided to design a plan of action against my life. My life had become a war zone for the enemy and his fallen angels. He began attacking me physically in many different ways. As I look back and ponder the first attack on my life (at age six), I remember I became extremely ill. My parents took me to the emergency room with a 106-degree temperature. I was examined, and the doctors diagnosed me with polio and placed my small, fragile body in this huge metal bed that completely surrounded me. This gigantic bed was called an iron lung. As time passed, I became worse. My temperature would not come down, so they carried me to a big stainless-steel bathtub filled with ice that was covered with a plastic sheet, and the nurses placed my white cotton sheet-wrapped body on the ice. I don't recall anything after that. My parents explained that after several hours of moving me from the tub of ice to the iron lung, my temperature finally lowered to 102 degrees. The following day it was determined I had chicken pox, mumps, and measles, all at the same time. When my temperature stabilized at 101 degrees, my parents were allowed to take me home. I missed three weeks of school and lost a lot of weight. I was already small in stature, and now I looked undernourished.

A lot happened to me in my first year as a Christian. Witnessing to others, the experience with the older man and his death, distributing tracts, taking piano lessons, and helping Mom with her Sunday school lessons as she would practice teaching her lesson to me before presenting it to her class. I basically received instruction in two different classes, my mom's and the class I attended. My foundation in Christ was nurtured as a child.

Then, Satan and his followers used others to attack my life during my sixth year. A young boy, around fourteen, invited me to play in his backyard. It was close to where we lived. I briefly shared this story in chapter 4. He built a tent out of lawn chairs and draped a quilt over them. We were playing house, and he told me to pretend I was sick. Then, he suggested we play doctor/patient. Of course, he was the doctor, and I was the patient. How convenient for the enemy to use innocent playtime to violate one of God's own children. I was rescued by my father's voice calling for me when he came home and found I was missing. If my father had not shown up when he did, I do not know what else might have happened. I felt relieved, although I had no understanding of what had transpired. Our heavenly Father calls us unto Him. If we know His voice, He will save us. When we hear His voice, we should recognize His voice and run to Him just like I did when I heard my Father's voice. Hearing his voice drew me to him and spared me from being harmed even more. I heard my father's voice, and I was obedient and ran to him.

The enemy works against us. He preys upon the young and innocent. God's Word says in 1 Peter 5:8 (Zondervan Life Application Bible), "Be self-controlled and alert. Your enemy, the devil, prowls around like a roaring lion looking for someone to devour." Zondervan's commentary explains this well: "Lions attack sick, young, or straggling animals; they choose victims who are alone or not alert. Peter warns us to watch out for Satan when we are suffering or being persecuted." I was young and naïve as a child would be, with not a clue of what had just transpired until years later. My mother was a new Christian and did not know about spiritual warfare. Once I was victimized, Satan opened a door of my innocent vulnerability to his attacks. This is how Satan operates. He takes advantage through deception and whatever means he can to destroy our lives and sometimes leave us in a state of confusion. This was the beginning of many attacks upon my life. He was angry at me because I allowed my Lord to use me as his vessel to spread His Word. After all, a man accepted Christ because of God working through me. Satan definitely wanted to wipe me out! However, Satan has no power over God's Children. We open that door through *sin*. It was years later that I understood how I unknowingly opened that door.

As time rolled on, my ministry for Jesus grew. I told everyone I saw about Jesus. Sometimes, I was laughed at, made fun of, and harassed. However, I did not let that hinder me. I gave my first tithe at the young age of six. My parents and I attended a tent meeting under the leadership of an evangelist who had a radio ministry. My parents always gave me dimes for my piggy bank, and I asked my mom what I should do with my piggy bank as it was full. She stated, "It is yours; you can do with it as you please. You can spend it, give it away, or just leave it in the piggy bank and decide later what you want to do with it." I told Mom I wanted to give it away. I took my bank of dimes with us on this trip. We arrived at the tent meeting, and during the message, the Holy Spirit impressed upon me to give all my dimes to this radio ministry pastor. At the end of the service, there was an altar call. I tugged on my mom's dress and told her I wanted to give my dimes to Jesus. Would she go with me to the front to take my piggy bank? She replied, "If you really want to do this, you must do this on your own. I will stay right here until you return." I walked down the long sawdust-covered aisle with my pink piggy bank clutched in my hands. I told the preacher I had a pink pig full of dimes, and I wanted to give them to Jesus. Tears began to roll down his cheeks as he hugged me and said, "Thank you, my child." He asked me my name, and I told him my name. He said, "Marylin, your gift has been received, and it will be used to reach and help young, troubled children across the southern United States." Wow, Jesus had used my offering, even though it was a small amount, to help other children.

One day, I was listening to the radio, and the preacher came on to minister to others. I said to Mom, "The camp meeting preacher is on the radio!" She said, "I am coming." Mom threw some pillows on the floor, and we stretched out on them to listen. He began sharing about a little girl named Marylin who gave a pink piggy bank at a camp meeting. I looked at Mom and smiled. He then said, "I do not eat pork, but this is one pig I definitely butchered! If the little girl is listening today, I want to thank her for that pig! The little pink pig had $50.00 in it!" I looked at Mom and said, "He's talking about the pig I gave him!" This was my first tithe. I gave all my savings to Jesus. Another way we tithe is by giving our time to the Lord. There are twenty-four hours in a day, and 10 percent of twenty-four hours is two hours and forty minutes daily.

Questions:

Have you ever tithed? At what age?

_____

Did you know Jesus as a child?

_____

How do you tithe your time?

_____

_____

_____

At the age of eight, I began playing the piano in church. We had no songbooks, and the song leader sang everything in the key of F or C. I started out plucking the melody, and then I prayed and asked God to show me how to put other notes with the melody line. He answered my prayer. I gradually began to play both hands together with no clue of what I was doing. I started piano lessons at the age of five. I played by ear and would go to my piano lessons and innocently ask my teacher to play my newly assigned songs. I wanted to know how they sounded so I could play them. I never thought about reading music or counting. My mother and I walked two miles one way to my piano lessons, so all the way home, I would hum what my teacher had played. By the time we were home, I had them all memorized and could sit at the piano and play them (without practicing and with no effort on my part). Therefore, I would not count, read the notes, etc. Needless to say, my teacher eventually caught on to what was happening, and one week, she said, "I think I'm going to let you work these up this week without playing them for you." I was in big trouble. I realized I couldn't read the notes; I could not count; I was lost without hearing the music! So, the following week, I could not play the new songs for her. I had to go back to square one and learn how to read notes, count, etc. This was really boring for me. I wanted to sit down at the piano and play! I enjoyed playing the piano at church because all I had to do was follow the song leader. I could use the gift God had given me. The ability to play by ear. This was great until I went to college and studied music. I did not know my theory, I did not understand the format of music, and I thought a "music degree" would be fun and easy. Was I ever wrong! My piano instructor made me learn classical music without hearing it first. I can remember the first summer break he gave me an eighteen-page Beethoven Sonata, and I had no clue as to how it sounded. He told me I was not allowed to buy the CD and listen to it. I worked on this piece all summer one measure at a time, counting and counting, looking at the phrasing and dynamics of the piece. I tried to understand the meaning of the piece, how did it flow, and what Beethoven was trying to express in this piece. When I went back the following fall semester, it was a huge stretch for me to play this Beethoven work without knowing how this piece sounded. I was extremely frustrated. As I played this piece for my instructor, he said, "Good job! He then put in the CD so I could hear it for the first time. I was surprised; I could recognize the piece I had just played. That was so strange for me to play it and then listen to it. All my life, I had depended on my "ear" to learn, and I never had to really work at my accomplishment in music before my college days. My instructor gave me music to learn on my own for six years. I was not allowed to hear anything I played until I had learned it on my own.

This is how some of us allow God to work in our lives. We can go on doing things our way and not take the time to learn or understand His way. If we will study God's Word and follow His instructions, He will help us through anything. Sometimes our way seems easier to us, and we do not work at living our lives the way God wants us to live. We do not search the Scriptures; we lean more on what we are told and what we "hear" from others. Maybe we do not "hear" what we need to practice in our own lives. We need to literally open the Bible and read so God can speak to us through His divine words. If we do not do this, we give Satan an open door to deceive us through our own thinking process and take advantage of our lack of knowledge. We have to have an instructor (the Holy Spirit) to teach us not to lean on what we hear or our own understanding. If we don't have God's Word in us, we can't fight the evil forces working against us. Therefore, we do not have the roots of the inspired Word of God within us. This is where tithing our time transpires fruit of knowledge and understanding. It is our responsibility to study God's Word, worship, praise, pray and have a relationship with our Father and His Son, Jesus. We have to remember, though, the only way to the Father is through Christ Jesus. We must study to show ourselves approved unto God. Second Timothy 2:15 (KJV): "Study to show thyself approved unto God, a workman that needeth not to be ashamed rightly dividing the word of truth."

Questions:

What do I do in my life that leads to strife, pain, hurt, fear, misunderstandings, and turmoil?

_____

_____

_____

Is there anything I can do to help me through these times?
Who do I lean on during these trying times?

_____

_____

_____

_____

Where am I going from here?

_____

_____

_____

Is what I am currently doing working in my life?

_____

_____

_____

_____

How can I change the patterns in my life?

_____

_____

_____

The first three years of elementary school were spent in a private Christian school; then, we moved, and elementary Christian education was not available in the area. I transferred to my first years of exposure to public education. It was so different. I really missed the inclusion of the Christian curriculum in my education. Parents, if at all possible, even if it takes great sacrifice, allow your children the experience of Christian education. It is so vitally important, especially in the times we are currently living. The Christians are already being persecuted; prayer out of the school setting and sports, along with other activities, have become so important that Christ is being set on the back burner, so to speak. God and His precious Son, Jesus, are not coming first in our lives anymore.

As I share my life, take the opportunity to reflect on your life. We may not even be aware of the priorities in our lives, and God can help us get our priorities straight. This process takes time to filter through. It has taken many years for me to work through all that my unfriendly contender has disconcertingly thrown my direction and some of the things that I allowed in my later years of life. My foundation was strong because of the loving determination my mother shared with me regarding Christ. A life she never experienced growing up. I believe her mission was to be my personal guide. That is how much God loves us. He provides what we need, and He promises never to leave us or forsake us. My mother's last words to me before she died were, "Marylin, my purpose in life was to teach you about Christ. God showed me when you were five years old that you were to share the Gospel with others. You are my precious little missionary." She also said, "She was blessed and honored to be chosen to be my mother." I feel honored that God cared enough for me to give me a beautiful, passionate, and loving mother who put Christ first in our lives. Thank You, Lord, for giving me a strong, devoted Christian mother. I am truly blessed beyond measure.

Questions to evaluate your support system.

How was your foundation formed?

_____

_____

_____

_____

Did you have a personal guide as you were growing up into maturity? What/who is the cornerstone in your life?

_____

_____

_____

_____

What/who has been in your life that caused roadblocks keeping you from building your foundation in your elementary years?

_____

_____

_____

_____

My elementary years were built on Christ, and He was the cornerstone of my life. That solid rock could not be destroyed. Satan threw many sledgehammers at my house and my foundation, my physical body (the house for the Holy Spirit), my mind, and my emotional being through many abusive situations, but he never conquered my heart or my spirit.

God has a plan for our protection, and I learned this really late in my life. My desire is to share with others how God helped me wade through the tidal waves and storms in my life. My spirit had been crushed but not beyond repair. My emotions were dynamited but not beyond repair. My physical body had been used as a punching bag, all battered and torn but not beyond repair. My mind has been tortured, confused at times, and beaten down to the point I couldn't think, but Jesus healed my body, soul, and spirit. Nothing is too big for God and His Son. God can do anything but fail. He is the ultimate healing power, and the repair he does is life-changing beyond anything we can imagine. My life was formed by God. Jeremiah 1:5a (Zondervan Life Application Bible): "Before I formed you in the womb I knew you, before you were born I set you apart." Isn't that awesome?! God knew me before He formed me. He knew the plans He had for me. He has a special plan and purpose for your life also. We were appointed by God for a specific reason before we were ever conceived. Wow! I am special. You are special. Jeremiah 29:11 (Zondervan Life Application Bible), "'For I know the plans I have for you,' declares the Lord, 'plans to prosper you and not to harm you, plans to give you hope and a future.'"

How many of us are who God created us to be from the beginning? Psalm 139 says that from the beginning, from the foundation of the world, God knew you. Before your parts were fashioned from the very dust of the earth, God knew you.

> For you created my inmost being; you knit me together in my mother's womb; I praise you because I am fearfully and wonderfully made; your works are wonderful. I know that full well. My frame was not hidden from you when I was made in the secret place. When I was woven together in the depth of the earth, your eyes saw my unformed body. All the days ordained for me were written in your book before one of them came to be.

> Psalm 139:13–16 (Zondervan Life Application Bible)

We are no accident. God's desire for you and me is to have a relationship with Him and His Son, Jesus Christ, and to be a viable part of His body on earth.

I am so thankful my mother encouraged me and taught me about God, Christ, and the Holy Spirit. The Holy Spirit and my mother were my teachers, and God was my leader. I learned at an early age to do what God wanted me to do. Then, Satan wanted to tempt/deceive me and try to stop me for many years, and I had no idea or understanding of how he wanted to destroy me; but we must remember he has no power unless we give it to him.

I studied hard in school and loved going to church. We attended a small mission-planted church, and I know belief in Jesus Christ, and my love for music sustained me throughout my teen years. God planted the words to the hymns inside my heart. I know my mother's love, the teaching of God's Word, the music, and my mother's prayers are what sustained my relationship with God throughout the abusive years.

God has brought me to a higher level in ministry. Since April of 2000, I have been participating in many avenues of ministry: the Homeless, Inter-City Mission Work, International and Domestic Missions, and Teen Pregnancy. I was also involved in Women's Prison Ministry, ministering to abused, battered women and raped and molested victims. God opened doors to minister to a few perpetrators as well. This year, I am in the process of starting a ministry for abused, battered, and crushed women and for victims of domestic violence. The statistics for domestic violence are high in the United States. Oklahoma, my home state, currently is number one in the nation for domestic violence. The stats are 49.1 percent of women in Oklahoma are in an abusive/domestic violence situation. In the United States, it is estimated that ten million people experience domestic violence in their homes each year.

The National Domestic Violence Hotline states "that over the years of experience offering 24/7 support, information, and advocacy for people in abusive relationships have been informed by the hard realities of domestic violence." Relationship abuse is ugly, even (and especially) when it comes from the people we love. The more informed we keep ourselves and others, the more prepared we will be to recognize and stop abuse when it happens. "On average, more than one in three women and one in four men in the US will experience rape, physical violence, and/or stalking by an intimate partner. One in ten high school students has experienced physical violence from a partner in the last year alone." Statistics like these demand that we all commit ourselves to end abuse for good.

Learn the facts about domestic violence in different situations. The statistics on this page have been compiled from various sources.

General Statistics

An average of twenty-four people per minute are victims of rape, physical violence, or stalking by an intimate partner in the United States—more than 12 million women and men over the course of a single year.

Nearly three in ten women (29 percent) and one in ten men (10 percent) in the US have experienced rape, physical violence, and/or stalking by a partner and reported it has a related impact on their functioning.

Just under 15 percent of women (14.8 percent) and 4 percent of men in the US have been injured as a result of intimate partner violence that included rape, physical violence, and/or stalking by an intimate partner.

One in four women (24.3 percent) and one in seven men

(13.8 percent) aged eighteen and older in the US have been the victim of severe physical violence by an intimate partner in their lifetime.

Intimate partner violence alone affects more than 12 million people every year.

Over one in three women (35.6 percent) and one in four men (28.5 percent) in the US have experienced rape, physical violence, and/or stalking by an intimate partner in their lifetime.

Almost half of all women and men in the US have experienced psychological aggression by an intimate partner in their lifetime (48.4 percent and 48.8 percent, respectively).

Women ages eighteen to twenty-four and twenty-five to thirty-four generally experience the highest rates of intimate partner violence.[3]

From 1994 to 2010, approximately four in five victims of intimate partner violence were female.[4]

Most female victims of intimate partner violence were previously victimized by the same offender at rates of 77 percent for women ages eighteen to twenty-four, 76 percent for ages twenty-five to thirty-four, and 81 percent for ages thirty-five to forty-nine.[5]

---

3 All the above statistics above were compiled and researched by Black, M. C., Basile, K. C., Breiding, M. J., Smith, S. G., Walters, M. L., Merrick, M. T., Chen, J., & Stevens, M. R. (2011). The National Intimate Partner and Sexual Violence Survey (NISVS): 2010 Summary Report. Atlanta, GA: National Center for Injury Prevention and Control, Centers for Disease Control and Prevention.

4 http://www.ncjrs.gov/App/publications/abstract.aspx?ID=261262

5 http://www.ncjrs.gov/App/publications/abstract.aspx?ID=261262

Nearly one in five women (18.3 percent) and one in seventy-one men (1.4 percent) have been raped in their lifetime.

Nearly one in ten women (9.4 percent) in the US have been raped by an intimate partner in their lifetime.

Eighty-one percent of women who experienced rape, stalking, or physical violence from an intimate partner reported significant impacts (short-term or long-term), like injuries or symptoms of post-traumatic stress disorder.

Thirty-five percent of men reported the same significant impacts from experiences of rape, stalking, or physical violence from an intimate partner.

More than half (51.1 percent) of female victims of rape reported being raped by an intimate partner; 40.8 percent reported being raped by an acquaintance.

For male victims, 52.4 percent reported being raped by an acquaintance; 15.1 percent reported being raped by a stranger.

Estimates suggest 13 percent of women and 6 percent of men will experience sexual coercion (unwanted sexual penetration after being pressured in a non-physical way) in their lifetime; 27.2 percent of women and 11.7 percent of men experience unwanted sexual contact.[6]

---

6 All the above statistics above were compiled and researched by Black, M. C., Basile, K. C., Breiding, M. J., Smith, S. G., Walters, M. L., Merrick, M. T., Chen, J., & Stevens, M. R. (2011). The National Intimate Partner and Sexual Violence Survey (NISVS): 2010 Summary Report. Atlanta, GA: National Center for Injury Prevention and Control, Centers for Disease Control and Prevention. End of statistics from National Domestic Violence Hotline.

There is a mighty work to do for God's kingdom. God tells us in His Word over 1,500 times to go and share the Gospel. Also, we are to minister to the poor, those who are sick, those who are in prison, those who are hungry, those who are in captivity, the children, widows, and all of God's creation. We can take what has been meant for bad and turn it around for good by helping those who are experiencing what we have been through. God is an awesome God! His love endures forever.

CHAPTER TEN
The Intimidation Journey: Bullies and Lies

We have to remember that our enemy comes to kill, steal our joy, steal our peace, steal our sanity, steal anything he can, and destroy our lives. He is cunning, he is a liar, he is cruel, and he will stop at nothing to try to destroy what God has ordained.

I was naïve and did not know wrong or mean behaviors in my home. My home was a safe place. The bullies, hurting, and unkind people were my unfriendly opponents. I did not know how to protect myself from these types of people. The saying that hurting people hurt others is true unless restoration is achieved in these victims' lives. Long-term effects will result from being bullied and abused or mistreated. Any crisis can change your life, but it is up to us to decide how we will accept these circumstances that we cannot change. Bullies have a fabricated personality. They are more afraid of you than you are of them; you just do not know it. The façade they project is there to protect their inadequacies, their fears, and their feeling of rejection. This is information I would have loved to have known when I was going through these stages of being bullied and abused in my younger life.

I matured physically at an early age and was teased a lot about my physique. This is one reason I loved the Christian school atmosphere. These unkind words were never spoken there. Fathers, be careful how you act and what you say in front of your sons. These behaviors and words are learned, and "these behaviors" scarred me for a very long time. I tried to hide my physique by wearing loose clothing, but I was required to tuck my shirts in at school, so that did not help. This defined the curves I had.

I had a coach in the seventh grade who made comments about my physical appearance. Some of the girls said they were compliments, but I was embarrassed by these comments and became ashamed of my body. Boys would sometimes hear the coach's remarks and repeat them to me, causing me more embarrassment. I finally got to the point I would make unkind remarks back at them. Such as "Shut up, stop teasing me." I now know the evil one was in the background, just loving it.

I did have many close friends who defended me, and one could say I was popular in school. But the few-minute harassers were powerful in my life. Their remarks had a great impact on me emotionally, spiritually, and relationally. They gave me the feeling of being controlled. No matter what I did or said, their remarks controlled my feelings. I did not know how to let what others said to me not affect me internally. The abusers in my life also left me feeling weak and controlled. I fought back the only way I knew how. The words I said back to them just seemed to go unheard. The kicks and fighting for my innocence from my perpetrators just appeared to be in vain. They changed nothing. These attacks still happened. These acts caused me to become passive. I gave my will over to people and had no choice but to do anything except what they said. It was almost like I became oppressed, thus giving my will to the devil without knowing I was doing this. I became shame-based and felt as if I deserved nothing. I came to the place where I did not even realize that I had a choice in anything. These choices were made for me. All I knew was to work hard and do my best. Smiling always seemed to help. I felt better when I smiled. Thus, I learned at an early age to smile and hide all the pain inside. No one would ever know the depth I repressed these abusive acts. I cosmetically camouflaged my entire feelings, and no one ever had a clue. In fact, my nickname was "Smiley."

God created us to be happy and feel good about ourselves. I would sing to myself the song, "I've got the joy, joy, joy, joy down in my heart!" The only sad thing about that was I did not know the difference between happiness and joy. I thought because I smiled all the time, I was happy and had this joy deep in my heart. An analogy for this feeling is to think about a person who is addicted to drugs or alcohol or food. Their pain is so intense that they feel they are compelled to get rid of their pain by feeling good or high. They use these vices to find comfort, even though it is only temporary. They are trying to fill a void in their lives; the need to be loved and accepted. If we do not have good feelings deep within our hearts, we will get these feelings from someone else or something else.

Questions regarding some of your experiences.

Did you feel protected from the world as you were growing up?

_____

_____

_____

_____

What kind of atmosphere were you around at school?

_____

_____

_____

_____

Was anyone unkind or verbally abusive to you?

_____

_____

_____

_____

Who and what did they say to you?

_____

_____

_____

_____

How did you handle it?

_____

_____

_____

_____

Were you a bully? If so, what did you say or do to be abusive to others?

_____

_____

_____

_____

As stated earlier, there are three ways we handle abuse. We either suppress it, repress it, or express it. I chose to repress it and pretend it was not there. So, what did this teach me? I learned to repress everything. My thoughts, my fears, my hurts, and my pain. By the time I reached my senior year, I was reluctant to share very much with anyone.

The spirit of fear became imbedded in my being. I had let fear enter my heart through the threats of my perpetrators. During these tender years of my life, I did not understand that fear could quench my faith and hope. The lack of biblical knowledge regarding how the enemy works in our lives hindered my ability to know where I was in the spiritual battle of principalities and powers. My enemy took advantage of my lack of knowledge in this area, but little did he know that God would turn all that he put upon me around for good. Later in life, I could use these circumstances to teach others how to recognize his tactics and ways. The only thing I knew to do at the time was to throw myself into sports and other activities. I played basketball, volleyball, and softball, participated in track, and anything I could to stay busy. School was easy for me; I never studied, and I learned quickly. I believe this is why I was interested in so many sports. I had to keep my mind occupied so as not to have time to think or feel. These are the things that I thought made me happy and feel accepted. I now know that these things are superficial. They do not last for eternity. They don't even last a lifetime. They are here today and gone tomorrow. The only real love and acceptance that last is God's love. The only real joy and happiness is the love of God for us. Who else do you know that would sacrifice their one and only Son for you? God's love for us is deeper than any valley, higher than the clouds, wider than the universe, and last forever and ever throughout all eternity. None of these other things matter in our lives. We need God, His Son, Jesus Christ, the Holy Spirit, and God's Word to have an abundant life. Open your heart today and allow Jesus to become the Lord of your life. Don't suffer another day. In 1 John 4:28, we learn that perfect love casts out fear. Only God can love perfectly and without fault. We must examine ourselves to see what we believe about God and His Son. We are loved unconditionally. First John 4:8 tells us that *God is love.*

Questions regarding mixed feelings of what was programmed in your life causing confusion.

What things made you feel important as a child?

_____

_____

_____

_____

Did you have any "vices" at an early age?

_____

_____

_____

_____

Did you learn to hide behind things so no one could see the pain inside? What was so painful that you felt you had to hide it?

_____

_____

_____

_____

_____

At what age did you begin to shape this pattern in your life?

_____

_____

_____

_____

_____

Can you see the mixed feelings one can acquire by how others' treatment toward you can impact your life? God's Word tells us not to be a stumbling block to others. What we do and say does have an impact on others. We must evaluate our actions and our verbal expressions. We are accountable for the way we treat others. Our enemy is an expert at drawing our attention from God's instruction. We can only fake not having pain for so long. What goes in must at some time come out, and the sooner, the better. Don't wait half a lifetime like I did. I want to share this with you, the reader, to help you get beyond your pain and live an abundant life so richly planned for you by our loving Father.

CHAPTER ELEVEN

The Journey to Victorious Living: "Jesus is the Answer through His Perfect Heart"

This is how I worked through the traumatic, victim, survivor, and thriver stages and learned to trust God's modality of living a victorious life through walking by faith and trusting in Him and His Son, Jesus Christ. We must plant Christ's love and God's Word in our hearts to obtain victory in our lives. This process takes a large amount of discipline and determination on our part. To work through these stages, we must look at what each phase consists of and recognize every part of the journey to be able to work through them.

The Stages Defined, paraphrased from the book *Counseling Victims of Sexual Abuse: The Three Stages of Healing*[7] (1. The Victim, 2. Survivor, 3. Thriver Stages),

> Trauma is when an individual has been assaulted in such a way they are not able to reset themselves. A person may have suffered from one trauma, or there may be layers of traumatic events in their life.
>
> 1. "Victim is one who is injured or subjected to suffering. This person will not seek help or therapy. They need to learn how to work through hurt, pain, rejection, sadness, anger,

---

7 From Cross Country University, Nashville, Tennessee, Seminar, Oklahoma City, Oklahoma.

and many other emotions. The victim looks for acceptance and love from others (relationships). When going through this stage, the person will have depression, withdraw from others, and have low self-esteem. The question usually asked in this stage is, 'How do I stay safe?'

2. "Survivor is striving to remain alive and to continue to live or exist beyond an event or occurrence. They find the means to live and exist in society by pushing themselves into survival mode. Some stay in this stage for years and may never progress through this level. This becomes a normal pattern, and they feel as if they are 'surviving the abuse/mistreatment.' The ways people learn to survive are by building walls around the pain, hurt, rejection, etc. Some may learn to survive through addictions such as alcohol, drugs, relationships, work, sex, pornography, food, and other vices that help them camouflage the pain. Basically, the survivor crawls their way through life and are in denial that a problem even exists. Some may distance themselves from others, and if they have been violated by an immediate family member, they may distance themselves from their perpetrator and their whole family. Most choose to be around others with similar past hurts, rejections, and addictions (friends), thus living in a web of deceit and being imprisoned within the self. Their attitude will shift from victim to survivor stage, and we must emphasize the necessity to seek God. True acceptance and realization of who God says I am needs to become a part of the thinking process. We need

to learn we are special, not who others say we are. Self-evaluation needs to transpire to work through this stage. The person experiencing the survivor stage must begin to identify emotional feelings and become aware of the things that have been programmed in their hearts and minds so as to not become stagnant so healing may take place.

3. "Thrive is when an individual grows, progresses toward goals, prospers, wants to be successful, wants to flourish, and grasps on to something aiming toward success. They have a desire to become who they are in Christ and choose to be around others who have overcome past hurts, rejections, addictions, etc. The thriver will choose others who handle situations in a positive way and will choose friends who encourage them and do not tear them down. They think about who they are as a person and about who God says they are. The steps to work through the victim mode, whether single trauma or multiple trauma, depends on if these stages have become layered. If they are layered, we may need a chisel or jackhammer to break through the victim/survival stages."

This writer wavered between the survivor/thriver stage for many years, being successful in some areas and not so successful in others. I chose to be around positive people and other Christians most of the time; however, sometimes, there was a need to be around those who had suffered abuse but not understanding why there was a feeling of empathy toward those who were hurting. God is so gracious, loving, and patient, waiting for the moment we are strong enough to endure and work through our pain.

I learned in my counseling sessions from my therapist, Delta Wilkinson, we all have triggers that need to be recognized so we may learn to control them. Examples of triggers include but are not limited to sounds, words spoken to us, smells, time of day, time of year, and/or wrong choice of friends. We have to control our thoughts/triggers, and we have to acquire knowledge and experience to recognize and break the cycle/patterns that the triggers allow us to follow.

I used a three-second rule. When a thought came to mind, I gave myself three seconds to quit entertaining the thought; if I didn't control the thought within three seconds, I may dwell on this thought, thus making it become reality or putting that thought into action. I needed to determine where these thoughts came from: God, self, or Satan. When I learned to recognize where these thoughts were coming from, I gained control over them. If I entertain my thoughts, I will be certain to fail. When a thought from self or Satan would immerge, it helped me to pound my fist in my hand and say, I refuse this thought, and I send it back where it came from—I will not entertain this thought. I have Jesus in my heart to help me control this thought. Philippians 4:13, "I can do all things through Christ who strengthens me." I will overcome the thoughts that are not of God. God also tells us to take every thought captive. We must learn to recognize the thought for what it is temptation. Temptation is not sin; it is only a way of checking us out. We must take our thoughts captive and cast them out of our mind before it becomes sin. God tells us to "take captive every thought to make it obedient to Christ" (2 Corinthians 10:5b). And Hebrews 4:12–13,

For the word of God is living and active. Sharper than

any double-edged sword, it penetrates even to dividing soul and spirit, joints, and marrow; it judges the thoughts and attitudes of the heart. Nothing in all creation is hidden from God's sight. Everything is uncovered and laid bare before the eyes of him to whom we must give account.

Hebrews 4:12–13
(Zondervan Life Application Bible)

We must know the tricks of the enemy. Thoughts that do not come from God may not come from us. Satan tries to convince us these thoughts are just our own innocent ideas. We need to be aware of and recognize the source. We must remember that the Holy Spirit brings conviction; guilt and condemnation come from the enemy. We must resist the devil, and he will flee. For it is written, "Get behind me, Satan."

If we follow through on a thought that is not of God, we must confess our sin to God so we may be forgiven, thus refusing to allow the thought or act of sin not to have a hold on us. The way to freedom from what the enemy tempts us with is through the perfect heart of God—His Son, Jesus Christ. Do not close your heart to God because of pain. We must keep our faith and not ever give up. If we will identify issues in our lives and take responsibility for what we have recognized, not blaming others or God, then we can repent from our thoughts/actions and receive restoration through the grace of God. Jesus died so we could have grace and forgiveness of sin. Give thanks and praise for this beautiful gift that comes straight from the perfect heart of God. What a blessing! God's perfect heart beats the perfect rhythm of life. We must strive to keep His heart in ours.

It is amazing how much baggage we carry around in our

lives. The following exercise, which I did in a women's group twenty years ago, is a good way to experience what it is like to carry this extra weight. Take one-inch by four-inches pieces of paper and write one item on each piece of paper about what issue you are carrying around in your mind and heart. For example: hurt, anger, pain, verbal abuse, emotional abuse, physical abuse, low self-esteem, bitterness, shame, strife, worry, alcohol addiction, food addiction, drug addiction, relationship addiction, sexual addiction, death of a loved one, divorce, abandonment, or whatever you are dealing with from your past and currently. Tape each piece of paper onto a sixteen-ounce can and place it in a paper sack. If you have identified ten different items, you will have ten sixteen-ounce cans in your sack (ten pounds). Carry this sack around with you everywhere you go for one day. How do you feel? Tired? Sluggish? Weak? Are you tired of lugging all of this baggage around? This is what you are doing to yourself on the inside. It is wearing you down to carry all of this load in your heart. It affects the way you feel, act, and think.

Jesus tells us in Matthew 11:28–30 to cast all of our cares (burdens) on him,

> Come unto me, all you who are weary and burdened, and I will give you rest. Take my yoke upon you and learn from me, for I am gentle and humble in heart, and you will find rest for your souls. For my yoke is easy and my burden is light.
>
> Matthew 11:28–30
> (Zondervan Life Application Bible)

A yoke is a heavy wooden harness that fits over the shoulders of an ox or oxen. It is attached to a piece of equipment the oxen are to pull. A person may be carrying heavy burdens of sin, excessive demands, oppression and persecution, and weariness in the search for God and healing. Jesus frees people from all these burdens. The rest that Jesus promises is love, healing, and peace with God. A relationship with God through Jesus Christ changes meaningless wearisome toil into spiritual productivity and purpose. In Matthew 11:28, this verse states Christ says to "learn of Me," how do we do this? Through the Word of God and prayer! We must develop a relationship with Him. We must be truthful with ourselves, especially if we have internalized these events. Admitting the truth is the best start to recovery we can do for ourselves. Fear is the root that causes us to keep the incidents secret. We must set ourselves free by sharing the facts with someone we trust. If you can't talk to anyone, begin by telling Jesus. He already knows all the facts, He is non-judgmental, and He will listen. Then, ask Him to give you guidance through the Holy Spirit. Read the Bible and allow God to speak to you through His Word.

I memorized scriptures to give me the strength to overcome and to replace thoughts that came from self and Satan. I had to take myself through a questioning process to evaluate my feelings. I had to learn what my triggers were and then have a plan of action to control the patterns they programmed.

There were certain times of the year when I thought I was depressed. I learned from my therapist, Delta, that depression, sadness, tiredness, and sickness have the same symptoms. So, the questioning process had to be established. I would ask myself questions along the lines of "Did something happen around this time of year that was traumatic to me?" "Are my feelings justified?" "Am I tired, sad, depressed, grieving, not feeling well?" If it was a date or time of year that I lost someone close to me, then the feeling of sadness or grief was normal. I wasn't depressed; I was sad. Getting in touch with these feelings and understanding why I felt the way I did gave me peace, and I would say to myself, "Marylin, it is okay to have these feelings. I would not be normal if I did not have them at this time." Then, the feeling would pass, and I could move forward. Now, I have peace knowing these feelings are natural because I know and understand the seasons of my life. I am "in touch" with the feelings that I have. Something as simple as understanding can be so rewarding and comforting. God gave me scriptures to help me through these feelings, and this is how we overcome the battles of our lives. We must renew our minds with God's Word to be victorious. We must trust God's ways and not lean on our own understanding. It takes work to have victory. God can heal our lives, not the things of the world. What is in the world is not of God. We must rely on His helping hand and strive to have the fruit of the Spirit in our lives. Galatians 5:22–23 (NIV) states this completely, "But the fruit of the Spirit is love, joy, peace, patience, kindness, goodness, faithfulness, gentleness, and self-control."

The fruit of the Spirit is the spontaneous work of the Holy Spirit in us. The Spirit produces these character traits that are found in the nature of Christ. They are the by-products of Christ's control—we can't obtain them by trying to get them without His help. Which of these qualities do you want the Spirit to produce in you?

If we want the fruit of the Spirit to grow in us, we must join our lives to His. We must know Him, love Him, remember Him, and imitate Him. Scripture tells us to make it our goal to be like Christ. Matthew 22:37–39 (KJV), "Jesus said unto him, Thou shalt love the Lord thy God with all thy heart, and with all thy soul, and with all thy mind. This is the first and great commandment. And the second is like unto it, Thou shalt love thy neighbor as thyself." As a result, we will fulfill the intended purpose of the first and second commandments, to love God and our neighbors. If we love ourselves, the rest will fall into place. If we don't love ourselves, how can we love others? This was a difficult assignment for me from my therapist. My first goal after working through all the abuse and everything that had me damaged emotionally, physically, mentally, and spiritually, and working through the forgiveness of others and forgiving of myself, I had to learn to love *me*. I had to find the person inside of me that God had created me to be. I believe that was my hardest assignment through the two years of therapy. Learning to love me.

Jesus is the answer to all of our situations through His perfect heart. This is the way to conquer all that life throws in our paths. We can only be victorious in and through Him. The Holy Spirit leads us into all truth and is able to bring many things to our remembrance. I received great relief and healing by recalling traumatic events in my life, dealing with them, and then taking the initiative to get on with my life. Sometimes, if memories have been shut out on purpose and embedded deep within the recesses of the mind, they will poison the entire system. The memories must be unlocked and exposed before wholeness can be established. Past memories must be released to God so that they don't entrap us, thus blocking freedom to enjoy the abundant life, now and in the future, that God has planned for us.

> Brothers, 'I do not consider myself yet to have taken hold of it. But one thing I do: Forgetting what is behind and straining toward what is ahead, I press on toward the goal to win the prize for which God has called me heavenward in Christ Jesus. All of us who are mature should take such a view of things. And if on some point you think differently, that too God will make clear to you.'
>
> Philippians 3:13–15
> (Zondervan Life Application Bible)

You were taught, with regard to your former way of life,

to put off your old self, which is being corrupted by its deceitful desires; to be made new in the attitude of your minds; and to put on the new self, created to be like God in true righteousness and holiness.

Ephesians 4:22–24
(Zondervan Life Application Bible)

Isaiah 43:18–19 (Zondervan Life Application Bible), "Forget the former things; do not dwell on the past. See, I am doing a new thing! Now it springs up; do you not perceive it? I am making a way in the wasteland."

It is important to remember that if this process is not done with the leadership and guidance of the Holy Spirit, it can be harmful and actually cause even more damage to already wounded emotions. Do not waste the most precious years of your life trying to do it your way. Seek God and His plan for your recovery. "He will not leave you or forsake you" (Hebrews 13:5). "He will lead you one step at a time and you will be transformed from glory to glory" (2 Corinthians 3:18). Put the Holy Spirit in charge of your memories. Allow Him the leadership in this area. If remembering something from your past is going to help you, then recall it. If it will not help you, or if the memory is not necessary for your healing, or if it would be harmful for you to remember, then be thankful you cannot recall it and believe that the Holy Spirit knows what you need to remember. Trust His leading. If you need help in this endeavor, seek ye first the kingdom of God through His Word to help in this process. Even though the Lord has promised never to leave us nor forsake us, do not go ahead without God, and do your own thing. Do not try to process more than you can handle. Make sure you are strong enough in the Lord to sustain the steps you need to work through. Pray diligently and steadfastly following the leading of the Holy Spirit. Sometimes, we must endure for a while, being patient and continuing in faith.

In chapter 1, I shared how I felt my spirit had been broken from all the abuse and all of the wrong that had been done to me. A broken spirit produces genuine sorrow. I had the sorrow of what had been done to me, sorrow for the sin I took upon myself through unforgiveness, sorrow for the sin of anger, sorrow for the repression I chose over facing the hurt, bitterness, self-pity, and all the emotions I endured and carried. To receive my healing, I had to take full responsibility for my part in allowing these emotions and actions (unforgiveness) into my life. My self-will had been shattered, and I did not know how to lift myself up from all that had been put on me. However, I did gain humility through the suffering and pain I endured. I had to continue to seek God and trust Him regardless of the appearance of the pain in my life. I had to keep my faith to survive. If I had not kept believing in God, Jesus Christ, and the Holy Spirit, I do not know where I would be today. God is real, and He will help us through the most devastating circumstances. We cannot lose sight of His promises to us. To have victory, we must continue to seek God, and we must be open to His teachings. When we finally say to ourselves that we do not have the answers to our problems, we must seek God for help. When I realized that my way was not working for me or helping me, I had to submit to my Father in heaven. He wanted to help me, but I had to totally submit my life to Him. I had to surrender all and let Jesus be the Lord of my life. The person who is broken in spirit does not demand; he/she asks. A person with a broken spirit will find joy in the morning, has a tender heart, gratitude for what others do, humility about themselves, and have gentleness in relating to others who have faults. God heals the broken-hearted. In Isaiah 57:15 (KJV), God declares that He will dwell "with him also that is of a contrite and humble spirit" (paraphrased).

When we experience brokenness, the blessings will follow, and then we will wonder why we resisted such joy and freedom for so long. God and His Son are the answer to our broken hearts. We may feel crushed for a season, but we must seek God's help, and He has given us the Holy Spirit for guidance and instruction. We must bond a relationship with Him through prayer and the reading of God's Word to attain victory. Christ always gives us the grace and the strength we need to go toward eventual victory. Trust God rather than question Him. It is not wrong to ask God why unless that questioning produces confusion. If you are confused, then ask God why and wait patiently for His answer and leadership through His Word and prayer. I can only testify of the great victory that Jesus Christ has given me through His redeeming blood, direction, grace, and mighty faithfulness. My victorious testimony came when I allowed Him to embrace me with His outstretched arms restoring me to the person He created me to be. Then, I could successfully overcome pain, hardship, abuse, mistreatment, rejection, betrayal, bondage, and opposition by allowing God, my loving Father, to show me the steps to take by appreciating and accepting Jesus Christ for His grace and mercy extended to me and following the guidance and leadership of the Holy Spirit. I confronted the causes of my hurt, pain, repressions, etc., and because the Holy Spirit led me to seek help to overcome my battles, I attained victory. Seek the Lord in your situation and follow the leading of the Holy Spirit. He will help you confront your own pain.

How do we continue to walk in victory? We must keep our focus on the "Light of our Life," Jesus Christ. We need to keep our temple filled with the Word of God and continue to praise and worship Him daily.

I will extol the Lord at all times, His praise will continually be on my lips. My soul will boast in the Lord; let the afflicted hear and rejoice. Glorify the Lord with me; let us exalt his name together. I sought the Lord, and he answered me; he delivered me from all my fears.

Psalm 34:1–4 (NIV)

This is one of my favorite scriptures that keeps me grounded when I need assurance. I will praise the Lord at *all* times. I have learned it takes a lot of discipline over and over again to praise Him at *all* times. It is important to fellowship with God our Father and His Son, Jesus Christ. Establish fellowship with positive, like-minded people.

We need to learn to hold every thought captive and keep our thoughts on God and His promises. Do not think about past traumas after working through these issues. Let go of these thoughts and keep your healing. Think positively about all things. "Whatever is true, whatever is noble, whatever is right, whatever is pure, whatever is lovely, whatever is admirable—if anything is excellent or praiseworthy—think on these things" (Philippians 4:8, NIV). Do not judge people for you know not what they have endured in their life. Be like Christ and love everyone for who they are. It is so important to observe others' actions without judging them. Learn to separate the sin from the person. God created everything good. It is our choices that are not good. God gave everyone free will, and we must have compassion for all of God's creation. It is not our place to pass judgment on anyone. It is God's commandment to love; therefore, we have to be obedient to His words in Matthew 7:1–2. "Do not judge, or you too will be judged. For in the same way you judge others, you will be judged, and with the measure you use, it will be measured to you." Zondervan's New Life Application Bible Commentary profoundly clarifies this passage:

Jesus tells us to examine our own motives and conduct instead of judging others. The traits that bother us in others are often the habits we dislike in ourselves. The untamed bad habits and behavior patterns are the very ones that we most want to change in others. Do you find it easy to magnify others' faults while excusing your own? If you are ready to criticize someone, check to see if you deserve the same criticism. Judge yourself first, and then lovingly forgive and help your neighbor.

Some are quick to judge those who have endured all forms of abuse. We have to obey God and be careful how we treat those who have tried to destroy themselves. God is merciful and just, and He wants us to love our neighbor as we love ourselves. Discern between good and evil by separating lies from God's truth. Choose God in everything. Make sure all things line up with God's Word, and replace all thoughts in your mind with what God says.

> Therefore, I urge you brothers, in view of God's mercy, to offer your bodies as living sacrifices, holy and pleasing to God—this is your spiritual act of worship. Do not conform any longer to the pattern of this world but be transformed by the renewing of your mind. Then you will be able to test and approve what God's will is—His good, pleasing, and perfect will.
>
> Romans 12:1–2 (NIV)

God's timing and ways are perfect. We must guard our

hearts against doubt, unbelief, and discouragement. The perfect way of the Father is to keep our faith, trust, and hope in Him. It is crucial to believe God's powerful words no matter what our earthly circumstances are. "I am the way, the truth, and the life" (John 14:6, KJV). Remember these words and plant them in your heart. "For we walk by faith and not by sight" (2 Corinthians 5:7, KJV). Remember the song, "Oh be careful little eyes what you see. Oh be careful little ears what you hear. Oh, be careful little feet where you go. Oh be careful little hands what you do." We must guard our eyes, ears, hands, and feet. Our eyes are the windows to our souls. We have to guard what we allow our eyes to see and our ears to hear, especially in this era that we currently live in. We must discern what kind of music, movies, television programs, radio programs we watch and listen to, and books we read because what we allow in our lives will eventually come out in some manner. Isaiah 33:15–16 says,

> He who walks righteously and speaks what is right, who rejects gain from extortion and keeps his hand from accepting bribes, who stops his ears against plots of murder and shuts his eyes against contemplating evil—this is the man who will dwell on the heights, whose refuge will be the mountain fortress. His bread will be supplied, and water will not fail him.
>
> Isaiah 33:15–16
> (Zondervan Life Application Bible)

Zondervan's commentary states, "These sinners realized that they could not live in the presence of the holy God, for He is like a fire that consumes evil. Only those who walk righteously and speak what is right can live with God through His

Son, Jesus." I ask God every day to help me walk righteously. Do I fail? Yes, but I pick myself up and start a new day in Him and ask Him for help. I am thankful that God gave His only begotten Son so that I may have forgiveness and a better life through Him with the leading of the Holy Spirit to help me each and every day to follow the example of Christ.

Remember, all good things come from God. James 1:17: "Every good and perfect gift is from above, coming down from the Father of the heavenly lights, who does not change like shifting shadows." Isaiah 26:3, "You will keep in perfect peace him whose mind is steadfast, because he trusts in you." Isaiah 42:10, "Sing to the Lord a new song, his praise from the ends of the earth you who go down to the sea, and all that is in it, you islands, and all who live in them." Second Corinthians 5:17, "Therefore, if anyone is in Christ, He is a new creation; the old has gone, the new has come!"

I pray this book has been an inspiration to you and given you the realization that God is a merciful God and He loves you. You are worthy of being free from all the enemy has brought against you. Trust in God's love, and He will deliver you from all your hurts, sorrow, and pain. I pray you discovered how God's Word is relevant to your everyday concerns and sufficient for creating wholeness and healing in your life. I pray you have been encouraged and comforted through the reading of this book and the scriptures provided, showing you how to apply the Word to your life as a guide to reaching new heights. I pray you will use the Word of God as a tool to affect your heart. You are God's beautiful child. You are worthy of being loved, accepted, and respected. Jesus died so you can have grace, joy, mercy, love, and peace. Accept His precious love and live your life abundantly in Him. Jesus is the answer for your life today. May God bless you continuously. Please write me a note if you need spiritual guidance. Victory is yours through Christ Jesus, our Lord!

Marylin Trent

Embracing Restoration Ministry Int'l, Inc.

P.O. Box 850574

Yukon, OK 73085

EmbracingRestoration@gmail.com

If the Holy Spirit touched your heart while reading and studying this book, please fill out the portion on the next page in the appropriate space and email it to me. Thank you for allowing me to share my testimony with you. May God give you peace.

Prayer: Father, I surrender my pain, hurts, past memories, and life to You; I want to serve You and ask You to be Lord of my life from this day forward. I choose to confess my sins, and I receive Your Son, Jesus Christ, in my life and ask You to give me eternal life. I confess with my mouth the Lord Jesus and believe in my heart that God hath raised Jesus Christ from the dead (Romans 9:10). This is a gift You provided for me through the sacrifice Your Son made for me. I accept this gift of love and chose this day to surrender everything to You. Jesus, I thank You for the precious blood You shed for me. Thank You for ascending into heaven so I may also ascend and be with You when You return. Thank You for providing a way for the Holy Spirit to come live in me, thus providing guidance and instruction over my life. Thank You for my healing, and I will praise Your name and worship You with all of my heart. I am Yours, and You are my Lord. Now, I submit myself to You, Jesus. Amen!

If you would like to be baptized, thus giving you a good conscience of God (1 Peter 3:21, KJV), and whoever believes and is baptized will be saved (Mark 16:16, KJV). Through baptism, I am buried therefore with Christ, by baptism into death, in order that, just as Christ was raised from the dead by the glory of the Father, I, too, might walk in newness of life (Romans 6:4). Jesus answered, "Truly, truly, I say to you, unless one is born of water and the Spirit, he cannot enter the kingdom of God" (John 3:5, KJV). Thank You, Jesus! Amen.

Name:

_____

Date I received healing and was set free:

_____

Date I believed, received, and became a new life in Jesus Christ:

_____

Date I was baptized:

_____

Please notify me if you need help in any area. God Bless! Rejoice!

To God be the *glory*! Amen!

Marylin Trent,

CEO/President

Embracing Restoration Ministries Int'l, INC.

P.O. Box 850574

Yukon, OK 73085

Email: EmbracingRestoration@gmail.com

ADDENDUM

The following information was taken from the website www.ipt-forensics.com for the purpose of educating everyone reading this book regarding this massive ongoing problem in our country today. I pray that more children can be protected through providing education regarding this topic. Please, study the following information because, through this article, someone may help a child who is being a victim of others' choices, whether it be sexual, emotional, physical, or verbal abuse. Pray for the protection of all children throughout the world.

Abstract: Lists of behavioral indicators for suspected sexual abuse have been widely publicized in the media and in the professional literature. The difficulty is that the problem behaviors claimed to be signs of sexual abuse are general signs of stress in children. To spread these lists without appropriate cautions and information about their limitations can generate confusion and mistakes. The same behavioral signs were used almost a century ago as behavioral signs for detecting masturbation in children.

One list of behavioral symptoms was published by the prestigious Journal of the American Medical Association (JAMA, 1985) and has been widely reprinted. We are advised to look for children who have one or more of the following behaviors:

become withdrawn and daydream excessively

evidence poor peer relationship

experience poor self-esteem

seem frightened or phobic, especially of adults

experience deterioration of body image

express general feelings of shame or guilt

exhibit a sudden deterioration in academic performance

show pseudo-mature personality development

attempt suicide

exhibit a positive relationship toward the offender

display regressive behavior

display enuresis (involuntary discharge of urine) and/or encopresis

engage in excessive masturbation

engage in highly sexualized play

become sexually promiscuous.

Here is another list of symptoms. This list is offered by Sgroi (1982):

overly compliant behavior

acting-out aggressive behavior

pseudo-mature behavior (not genuine or sincere—acting like an adult)

hints about sexual activity

persistent and inappropriate sexual play with peers or toys or with themselves

sexually aggressive behavior with others

detailed and age-inappropriate understanding of sexual behavior

arriving early at school or leaving late with few, if any, absences

poor peer relationships or inability to make friends

lack of trust, particularly with significant others

nonparticipation in school and school activities

inability to concentrate m school

sudden drop in school performance

extraordinary fear of males, of strangers, or of being left alone

complaints of fatigue or physical illness, which could mask depression

low self-esteem.

There is some agreement between these two lists, such as problems with various fears, peer relationships, and sexual knowledge or activity that seem beyond a young child's years. There are also symptoms that appear on one list but not the other, such as daydreaming, depression, and being too compliant. We might decide that behaviors found on both lists are better indicators of sexual abuse than those found on only one. Or, if a child shows many symptoms rather than only one, perhaps that fact should strengthen our faith in the diagnosis of abuse. Unfortunately, there is no evidence that either of these strategies will be effective.

The task of detecting abuse is made more difficult because these two lists, long as they are, are not exhaustive. A survey of many such compilations proposed by various experts (Cohen, 1985) adds the following behavioral signs to those listed above:

loss of appetite

clinging to a parent

tics (muscle twitch, quirk of behavior)

hypervigilance

running away

irritability

difficulty with eye contact

hyperactivity

extreme interest in fire

unprovoked crying

taking an excessive number of baths

suspiciousness

sleepwalking

sudden massive weight gain or loss

excessive urination

medical conditions such as pneumonia or mononucleosis

confusion

nightmares

a poor mother-daughter relationship

overdependency.

At this point, it seems that nearly every problem behavior ever detected in children has been offered by someone as a sign of child sexual abuse. The problem is the high probability that any normal child might, at some point in childhood, exhibit one or more of these behaviors and thereby risk being perceived as an abuse victim. To spread these lists of behavioral indicators without appropriate caution and information about their limitations can generate mistakes, confusion, over-reaction, and over-interpretation.

Note the following list of children's behaviors:

depression

overly dependent behavior

aggression

whining

demanding

lack of affectionate behaviors

feminine (passive) aggressiveness

encopresis

anxiety

neurotic problems

anxiety about sexual matters

problems of both over- and under-control.

These symptoms, however, are not claimed as signs of child sexual abuse but as behaviors indicative of parental conflict in the home that may or may not lead to divorce (Emery, 1982). Many of these symptoms overlap with the suggested signs of sexual abuse. Neurotic problems could subsume a variety of fears, depression might manifest itself in withdrawal or other signs of sadness, and over-control could look a lot like pseudo-maturity.

The cautions about suggested behavioral signs do not mean that adults should not try to identify and aid children who show signs of distress. A sensitive and caring adult who notices problem behaviors by a child will want to try to find out what is wrong. But the adult must keep an open mind about what might be troubling the child and must be careful about the nature of the questions asked. A rush to judgment and premature closure on sexual abuse as a cause of the problems behaviors should be avoided. The odds are against this diagnosis.

Among others, J. Kellogg, MD, originator of cornflakes, produced several manuals for parents to help them stamp out the evil of masturbation. In his books, he listed behavioral signs for parents to be alert for in order to determine whether their child was masturbating (Money, 1985). These behavioral signs for masturbation included the following (current suggested behavioral indicators for sexual abuse are in italics):

general debility, including exhaustion *(complaints of fatigue or physical illness which could mask depression)*

sudden change in disposition *(display regressive behavior)*

lassitude, dislike for play, and lifelessness *(become withdrawn and daydream excessively)*

sleeplessness *(nightmares; sleepwalking)*

failure of mental capacity *(sudden deterioration in academic performance; inability to concentrate in school; sudden drop in school performance)*

untrustworthiness *(poor peer relationships or inability to make friends; acting-out aggressive behavior; lack of trust, particularly with significant others)*

love of solitude *(become withdrawn and daydream excessively)*

bashfulness *(seems frightened or phobic, especially*

of adults)

unnatural boldness *(acting-out aggressive behavior; persistent and inappropriate sexual play with peers or toys or with themselves; become sexually promiscuous)*

easily frightened *(seems frightened or phobic, especially of adults)*

confusion of ideas (including vulgar joking) *(confusion; hints about sexual activity)*

capricious appetite *(sudden massive weight gain or loss)*

unnatural paleness *(experience deterioration of body image; complaints of fatigue or physical illness which could mask depression)*

wetting the bed *(display enuresis and/or encopresis; excessive urination)*

unchastity of speech, including fondness for obscene stories *(hints about sexual activity; engage in highly sexualized play)*

early symptoms of consumption, or what are supposed to be such, including cough, short breathing, and soreness of the lungs *(medical conditions such as pneumonia or mononucleosis)*

The behavioral indicators parents could use then to know if their children were masturbating are the same behavioral indicators now said to suggest that a child has been sexually abused. John Money (1985) states Kellogg's listing of suspicious signs has been given a new lease on life currently by the professional detectives of sexual child abuse. Here is an example of those who have not learned from history being condemned to repeat it, replete with all its dreadful consequences (1997).

The cautions about suggested behavioral signs do not mean that adults should not try to identify and aid children who show signs of distress. A sensitive and caring adult who notices problem behaviors by a child will want to try to find out what is wrong. But the adult must keep an open mind about what might be troubling the child and must be careful about the nature of the questions asked. A rush to judgment and premature closure on sexual abuse as a cause of the problems behaviors should be avoided. The odds are against this diagnosis.[8]

---

8 Ross Legrand, Hollida Wakefield, and Ralph Under-wager are psychologists at the Institute for Psychological Therapies, 2344 Nicollet Avenue South, Suite 170, Minneapolis, Minnesota 55404. This article is taken from The Real World of Child Interrogations, by Ralph Underwager and Hollida Wakefield, C. C. Thomas, in press.

REFERENCES

AMA diagnostic and treatment guidelines concerning child abuse and neglect. *Journal of the American Medical Association*, 254, 1985, 796–800.

American Psychiatric Association *Diagnostic and Statistical Manual of Mental Disorders* (3rd Edition-Revised), Washington, DC: Author, 1987.

Besharov, D. J. Paper given at the VOCAL (Victims of Child Abuse Laws), National Convention, Minneapolis, Minnesota, 1985.

Cohen, A. The unreliability of expert testimony on the typical characteristics of sexual abuse victims. *Georgetown Law Journal*, 74, 1985, 429–456.

Emery, R. E. Interparental conflict and the children of discord and divorce. *Psychological Bulletin*, 92, 1982, 310–330.

Gundersen, B. H., Melas, P. S., and Skar, J. E. Sexual behavior in preschool children: Teachers' observations. In L. L. Constantine & F. M. Martinson (Eds.), *Children and Sex: New Findings, New Perspectives*, 45–51. Boston: Little, Brown & Company, 1981.

Hughes, H. M. & Barad, S. J. Psychological functioning of children in a battered woman's shelter: A preliminary investigation. *American Journal of Orthopsychiatry*, 53, 1983, 525–531.

Jaffe, P., Wolfe, D., Wilson, S., and Zak, L. Similarities in behavioral and social maladjustment among child victims and witnesses to family violence. *American Journal of Orthopsychiatry*, 56, 1986, 142–146.

Martinson, F. M. Eroticism in infancy and childhood. In L. L. Constantine & F. M. Martinson (Eds.), *Children and Sex: New Findings, New Perspectives*, 23–35). Boston: Little, Brown & Company, 1981.

Money, J. *Destroying Angels*. Buffalo, New York: Prometheus Books, 1985.

NCCAN (National Center on Child Abuse and Neglect) Executive summary: National study of the incidence and severity of child abuse and neglect, National Center on Child Abuse and Neglect. (DDHS Publication No.81–30329). Washington, DC: U.S. Government Printing Office, 1981a.

NCCAN (National Center on Child Abuse and Neglect) Study findings: National study of the incidence and severity of child abuse and neglect, National Center on Child Abuse and Neglect. (DDHS Publication No.81–30325). Washington, DC: U.S. Government Printing Office, 1981b.

Porter, B. and O'Leary, D. Marital discord and childhood behavior problems. *Journal of Abnormal Psychology*, 8, 1980, 287–195.

Sgroi, S. M. *Handbook of Clinical Intervention in Child Sexual Abuse*. Lexington, MA: Lexington Books, 1982.

Wakefield, H., and Underwager, R. *Accusations of Child Sexual Abuse*. Springfield, IL: Charles C. Thomas, 1988.

Wallerstein, J. S., and Kelly, J. B. *Surviving the Breakup: How Children and Parents Cope with Divorce*. New York: Basic Books, 1980.

Wolman, B. (Ed.) *Handbook of Developmental Psychology*. Englewood Cliffs, NJ: Prentice-Hall, 1983.

Ross Legrand, Hollida Wakefield, and Ralph Under-wager are psychologists at the Institute for Psychological Therapies, 2344 Nicollet Avenue South, Suite 170, Minneapolis, Minnesota 55404. This article is taken from The Real World of Child Interrogations by Ralph Underwager and Hollida Wakefield, C. C. Thomas, in press.

Printed in the USA
CPSIA information can be obtained
at www.ICGtesting.com
LVHW060959270124
769471LV00163B/3781